2 JESUS SAVES

10 NOT ASHAMED

17 THE WAY

26 MIGHTY TO SAVE

33 WE CRY OUT

40 YOU ARE THE LORD

47 EVERLASTING GOD

52 OVERCOME

63 YOU NEVER LET GO

70 UNRESTRAINED

75 KING JESUS

ISBN 978-1-4234-9985-5

WORSHIP TOGETHER

HAL·LEONARD® CORPORATION

7777 W. BLUEMOUND RD. P.O. BOX 13819 MILWAUKEE, WI 53213

Visit Hal Leonard Online at
www.halleonard.com

Jesus Saves

Capo 4 (G)

Words and Music by
TIM HUGHES
and NICK HERBERT

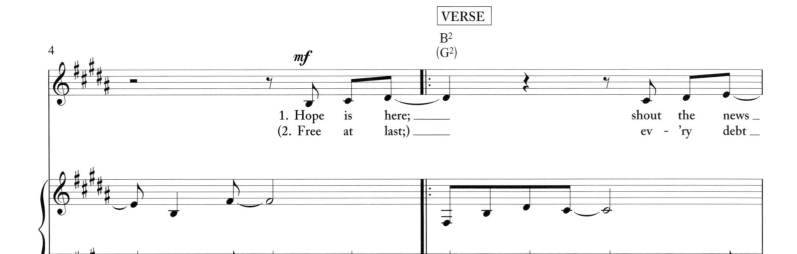

VERSE

1. Hope is here; ___ shout the news ___
(2. Free at last;) ___ ev - 'ry debt ___

___ to ev - 'ry - one. ___ It's a new ___
___ has been ___ re - paid, ___ bro - ken hearts ___

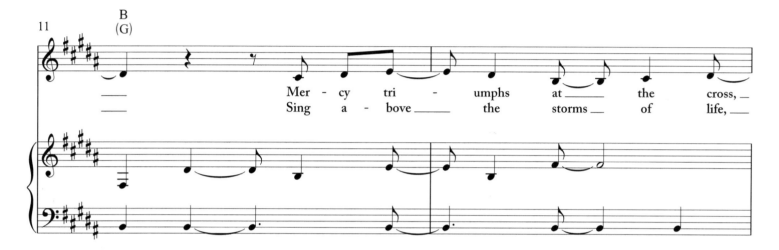

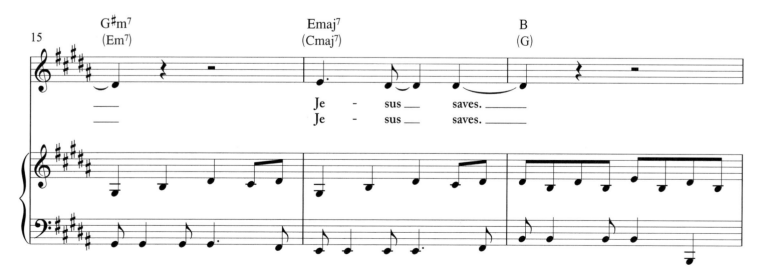

Raise a shout _____ to let all the world _ know that

Je - sus _ saves! _____ 2. Free at last; _ ___ Sing _ it out _
Shout _ it out _

Fill back in 2nd time

_____ to let all the world _ know that

Je - sus _ saves! _____ Raise a shout _

2nd time to Coda

to let all the world know that Je - sus saves!

BRIDGE

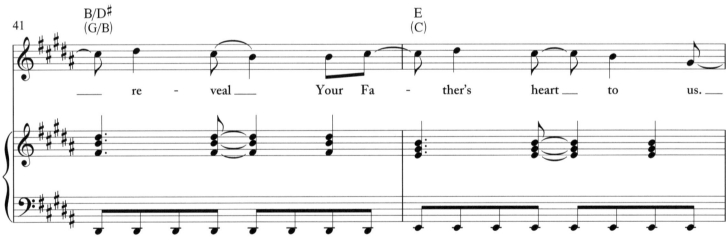

You save, You heal, re - store,

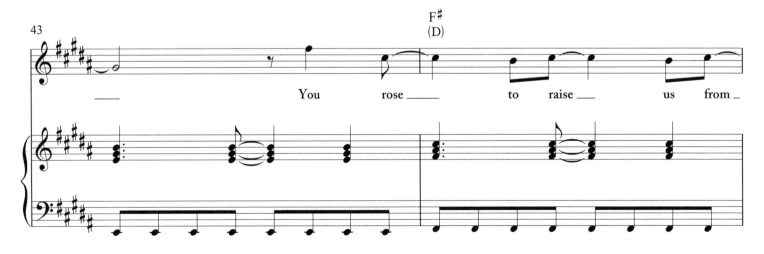

re - veal Your Fa - ther's heart to us.

You rose to raise us from

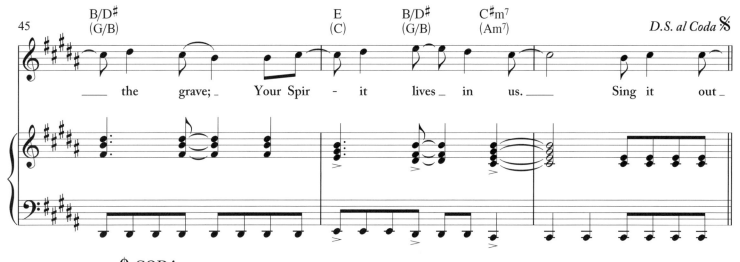

D.S. al Coda 𝄋

the grave; Your Spir - it lives in us. Sing it out

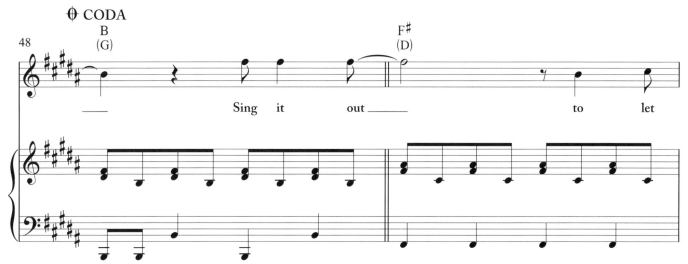

CODA

Sing it out to let

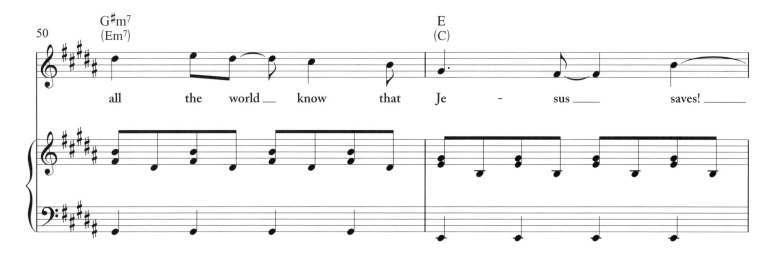

all the world know that Je - sus saves!

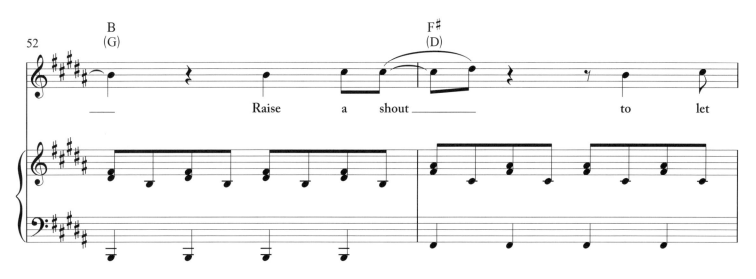

Raise a shout to let

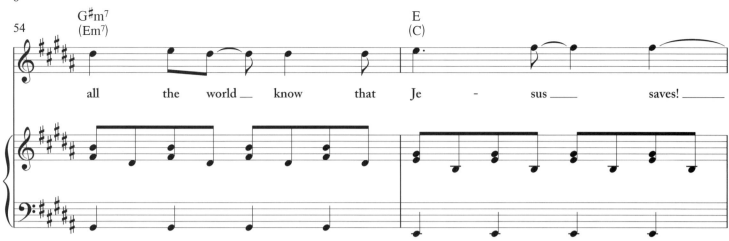

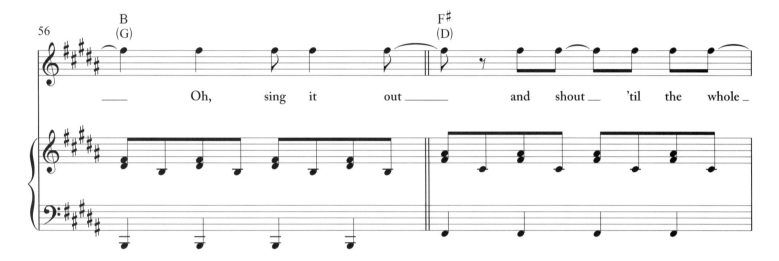

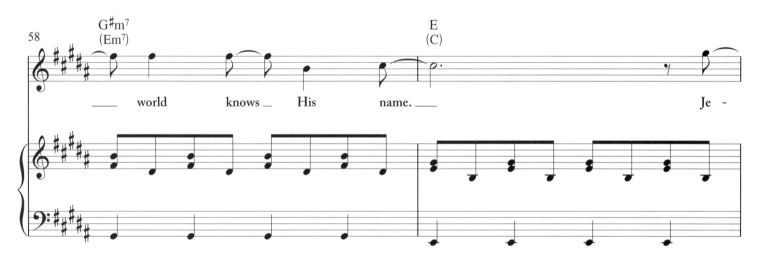

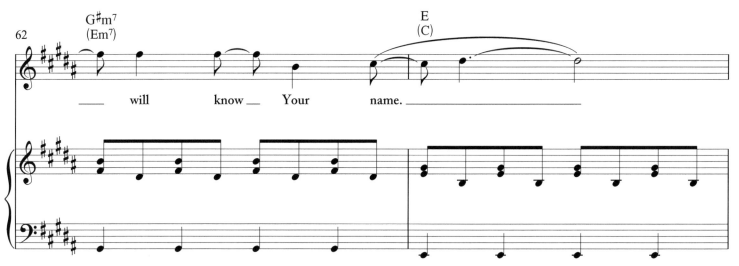

will know Your name.

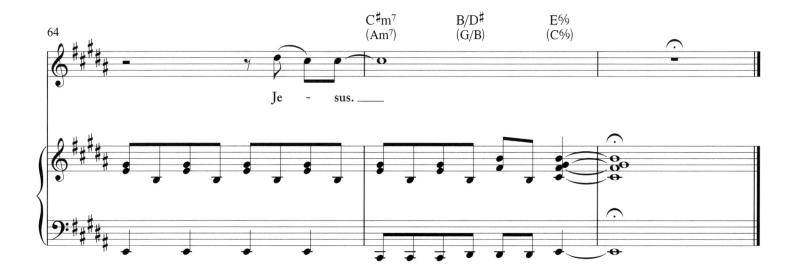

Je - sus.

Chords Used in This Song

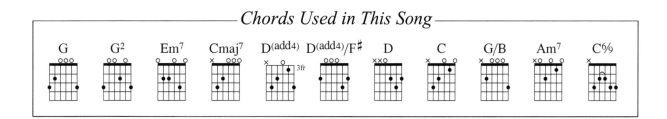

G G2 Em7 Cmaj7 D(add4) D(add4)/F♯ D C G/B Am7 C6/9

Not Ashamed

Words and Music by
JEREMY CAMP
and JON EGAN

Capo 4 (G)

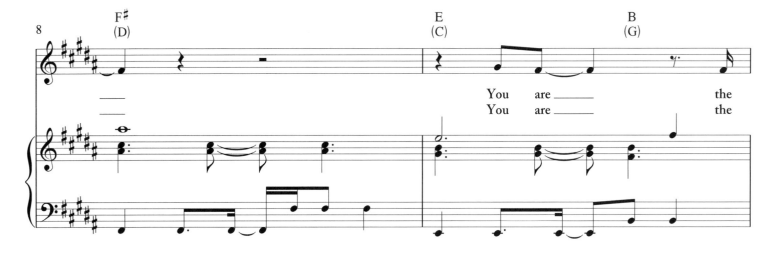

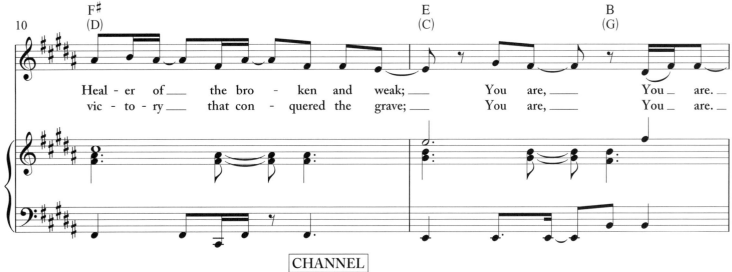

CHANNEL

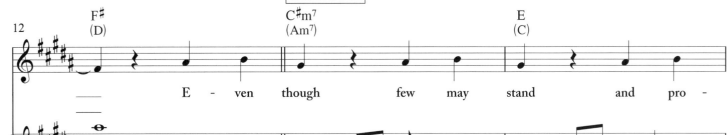

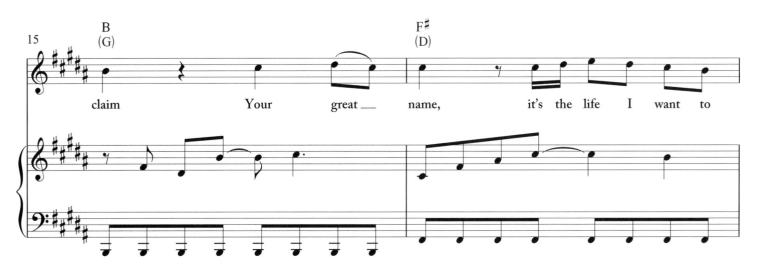

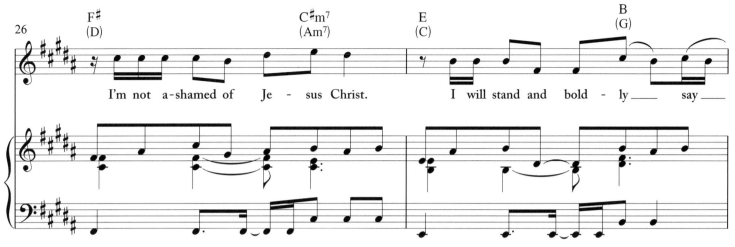

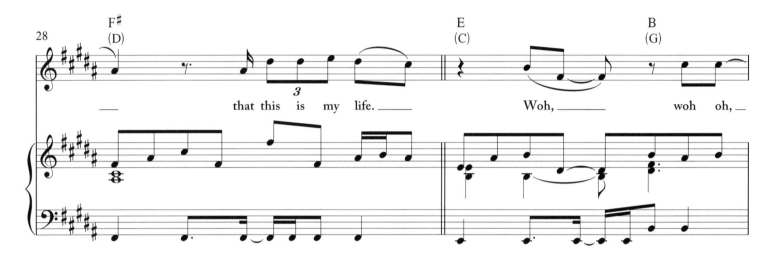

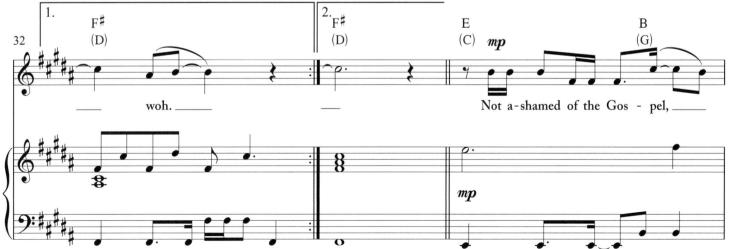

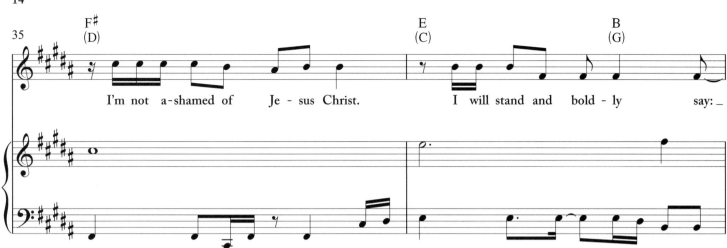

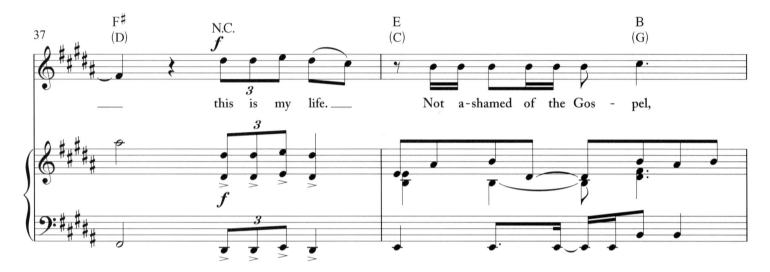

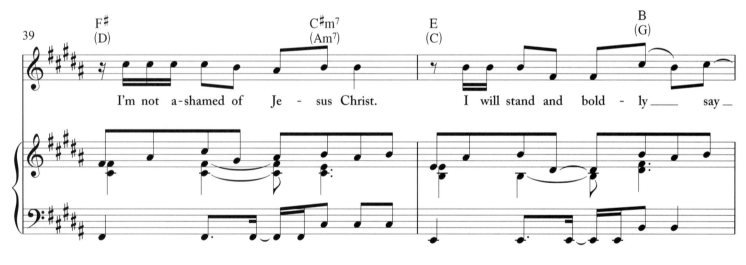

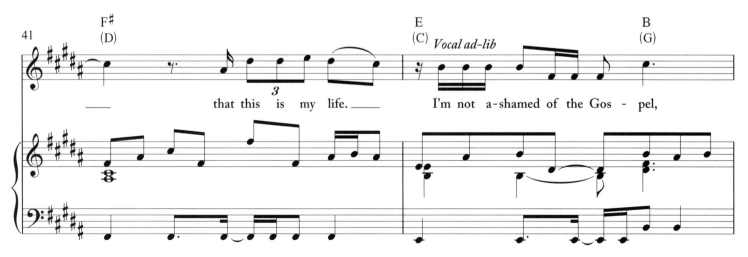

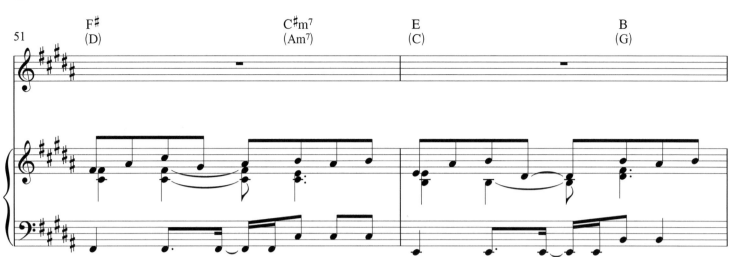

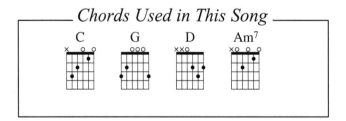

The Way

Words and Music by
JEREMY CAMP, BRAD PEENS,
ROB WILLIAMS, and GRANT DRYDEN

wis - dom, You___ al - ways an - swer and give the words___ of life,___

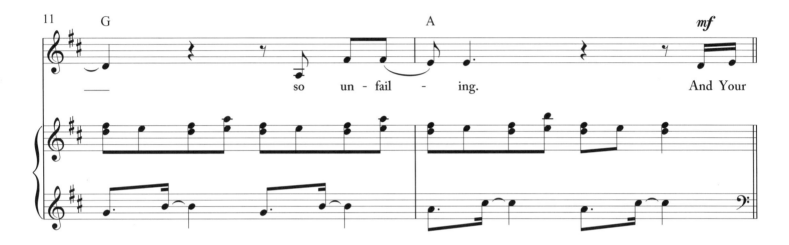

___ so un - fail - ing. And Your

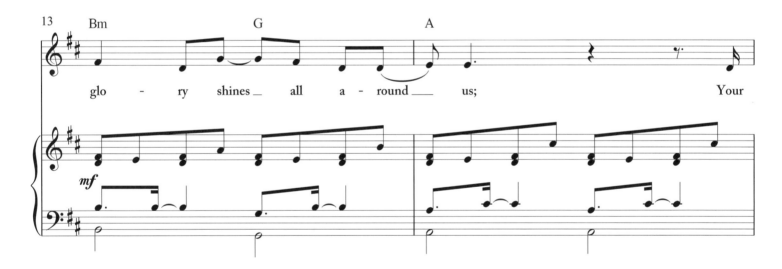

glo - ry shines___ all a - round___ us; Your

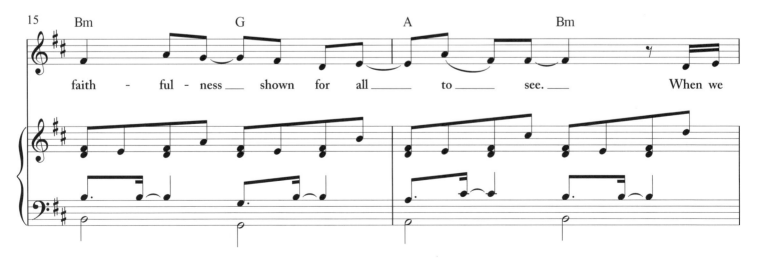

faith - ful - ness___ shown for all_____ to_____ see.___ When we

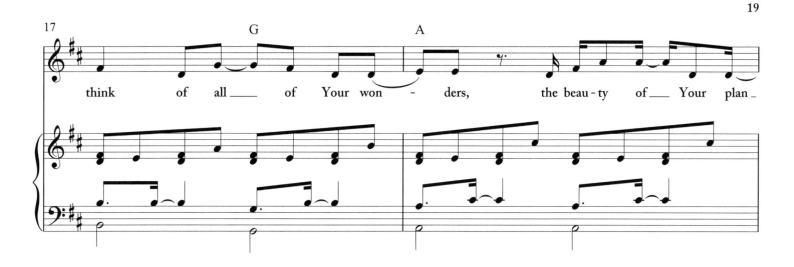

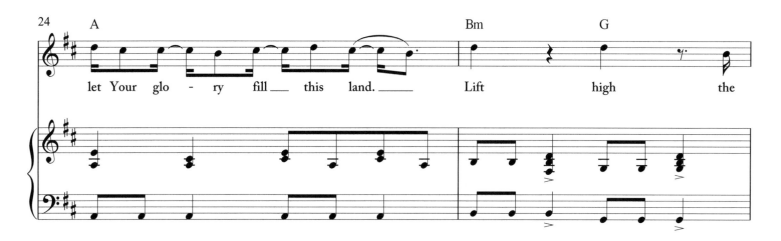

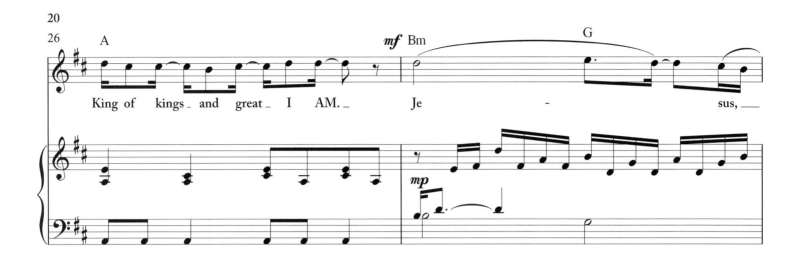

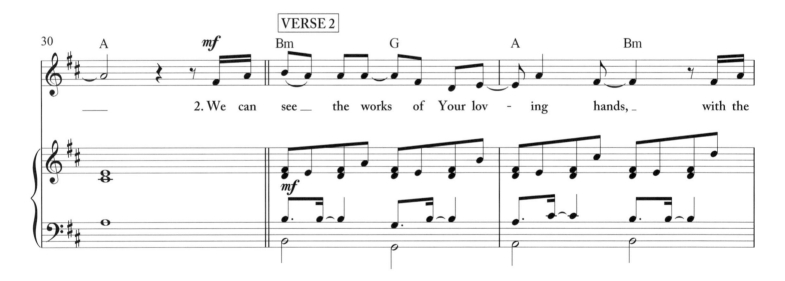

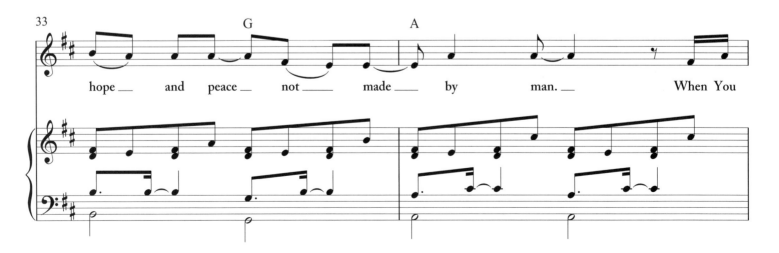

poured out Your grace ___ and Your mer - cy, and You held out ___ Your arms ___

___ so we ___ could see; ___ You bled for all ___ man - kind, ___

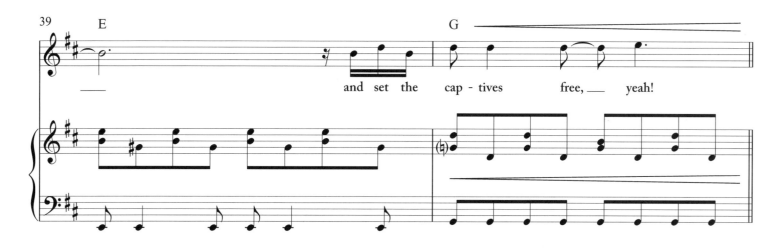

___ and set the cap - tives free, ___ yeah!

CHORUS

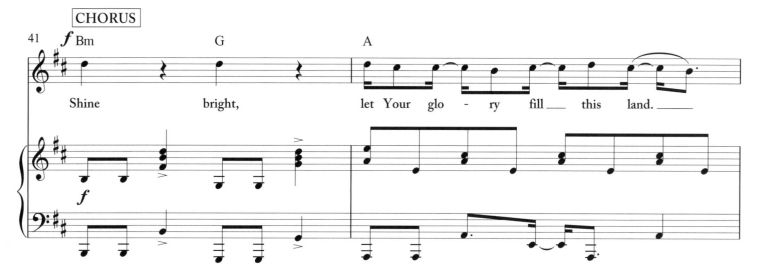

Shine bright, let Your glo - ry fill ___ this land. ___

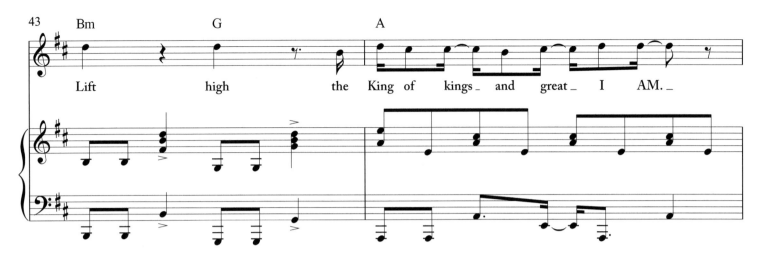

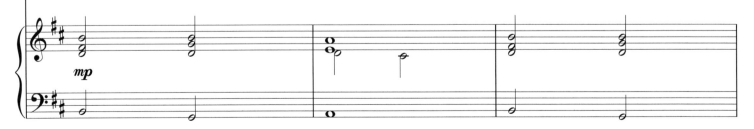

You are __ the Way. __ Na na na na na nah, __ Je - sus. __

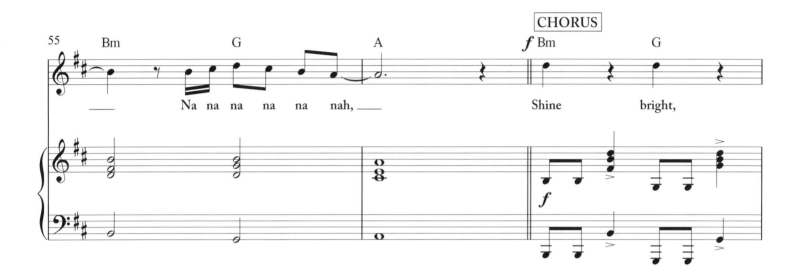

CHORUS

Na na na na na nah, __ Shine bright,

let Your glo - ry fill __ this land. __ Lift high the

King of kings, and great __ I AM! __ Shine bright,

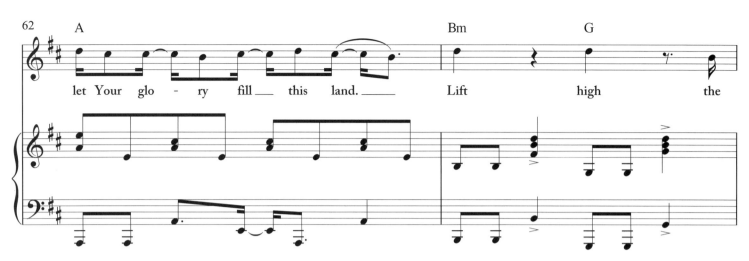

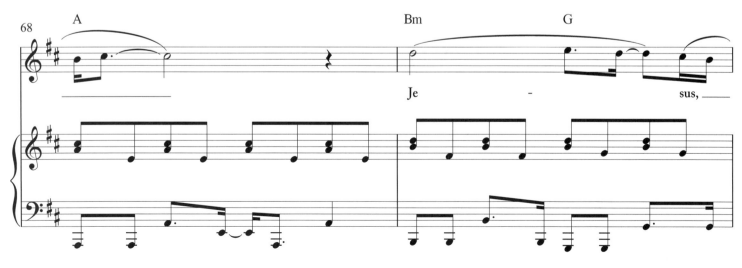

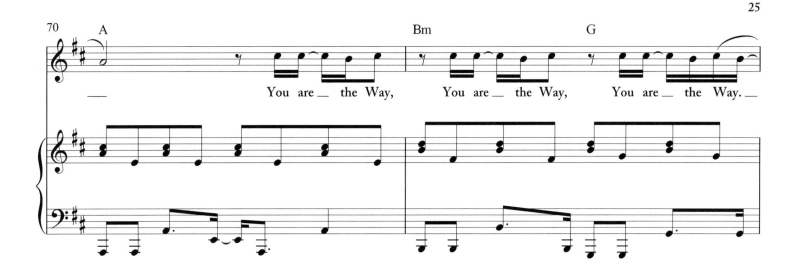

You are __ the Way, You are __ the Way, You are __ the Way. __

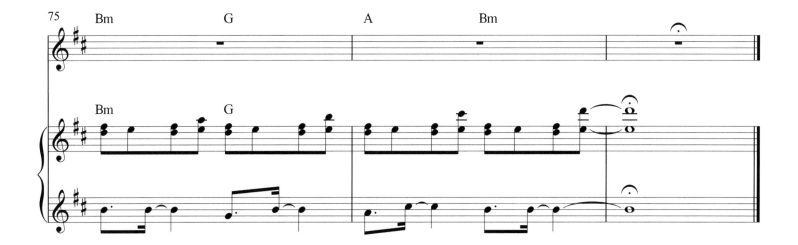

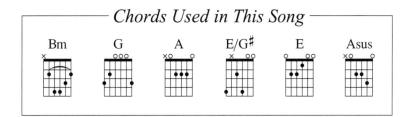

Chords Used in This Song

Bm G A E/G# E Asus

Mighty to Save

Words and Music by
BEN FIELDING
and REUBEN MORGAN

Capo 1 (G)

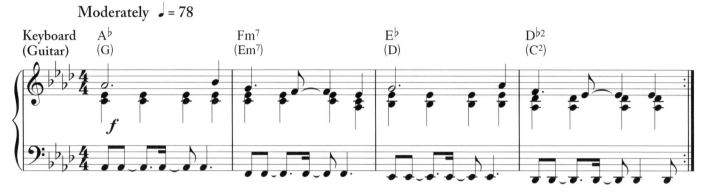

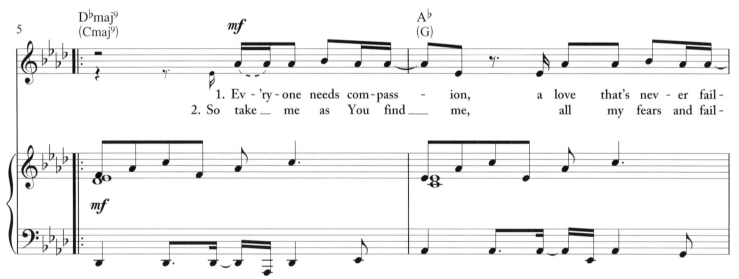

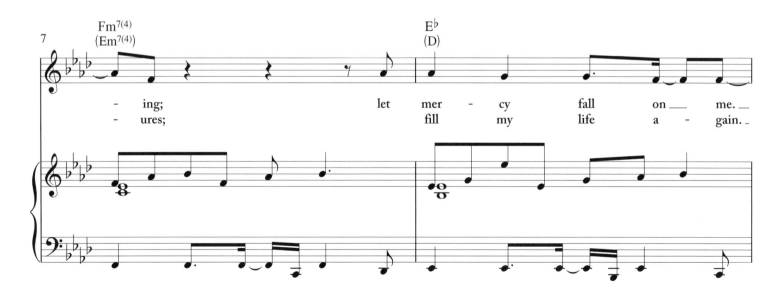

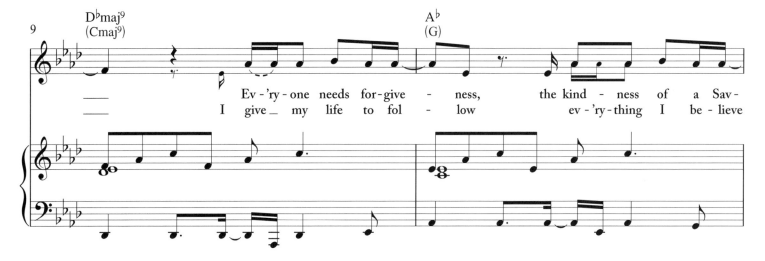

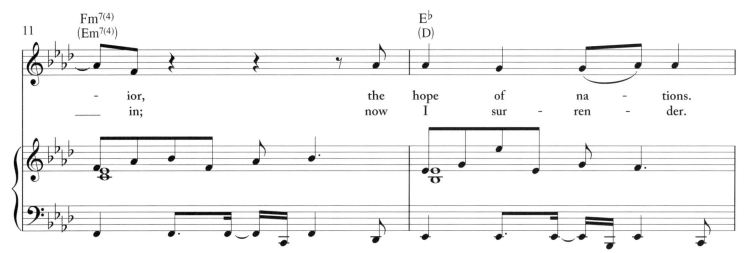

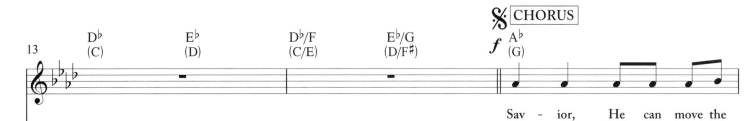

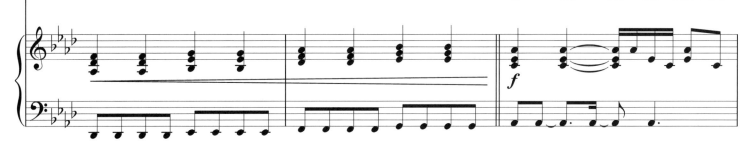

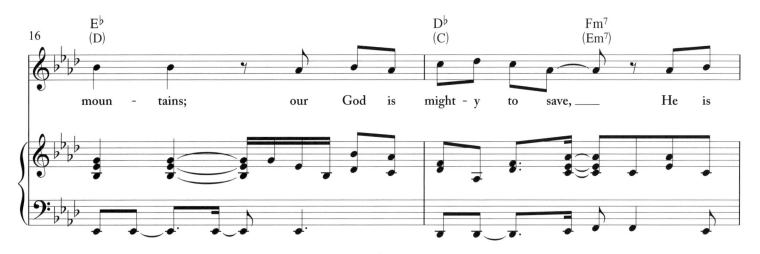

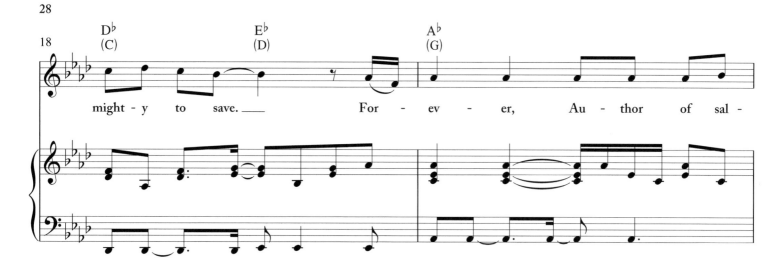

might-y to save. ___ For - ev - er, Au - thor of sal -

va - tion; He rose and con - quered the grave, ___ Je - sus

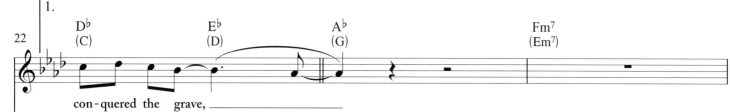

con - quered the grave, ___

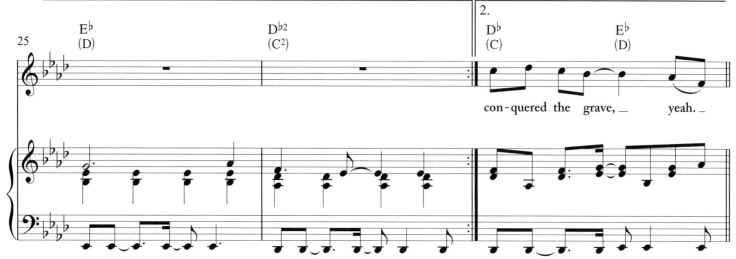

con - quered the grave, _ yeah. _

BRIDGE

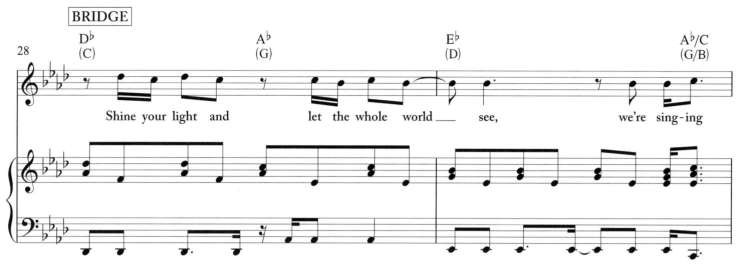

Shine your light and let the whole world ___ see, we're sing-ing

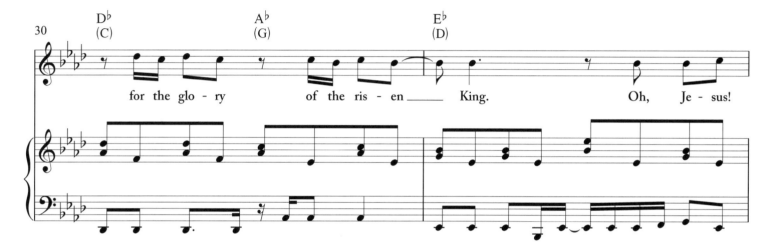

for the glo - ry of the ris - en ___ King. Oh, Je - sus!

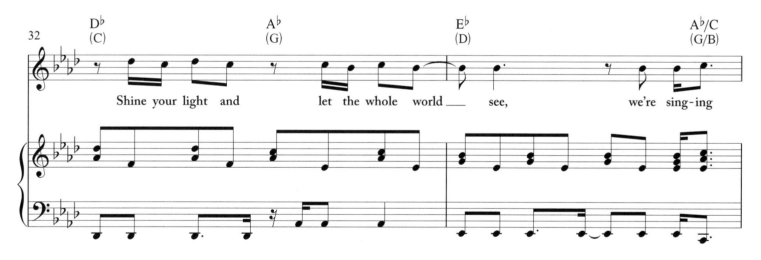

Shine your light and let the whole world ___ see, we're sing-ing

D.S. al Coda 𝄋

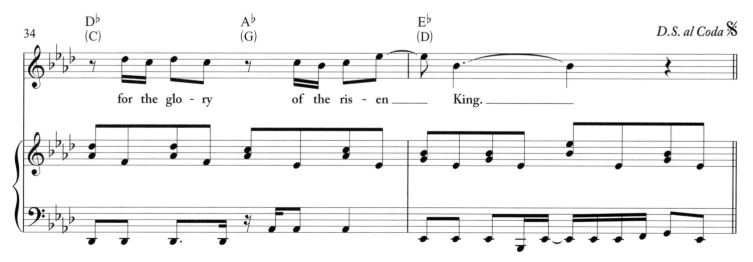

for the glo - ry of the ris - en ___ King. ___

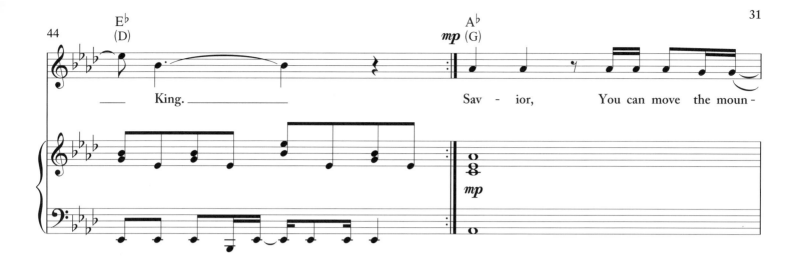

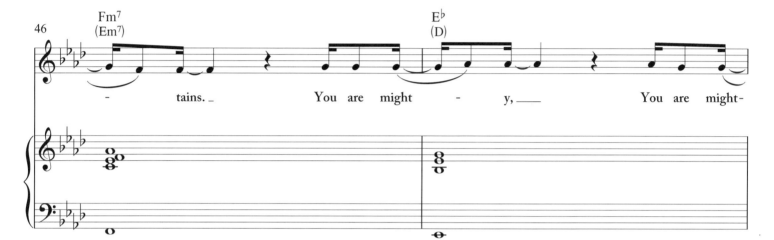

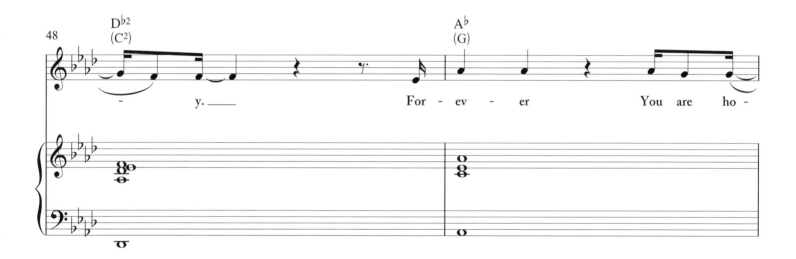

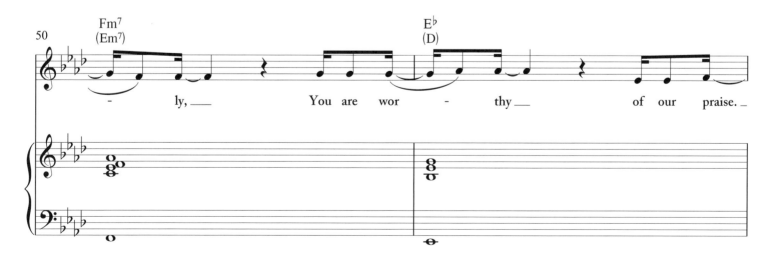

Chords Used in This Song

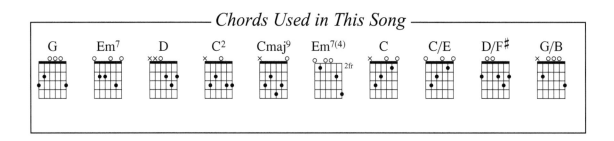

We Cry Out

Words and Music by
JEREMY CAMP
and BRENTON BROWN

they tell of ___ Your glo - ry. ___

VERSE 2, 3

2. We who called up - on Your name can - not be si - lent;
3. In - to all the world we take the mys - t'ry of Your

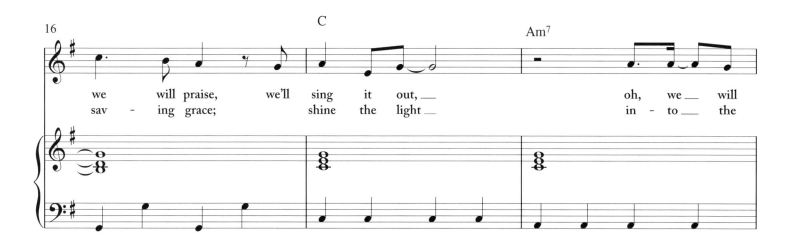

we will praise, we'll sing it out, ___ oh, we ___ will
sav - ing grace; shine the light ___ in - to ___ the

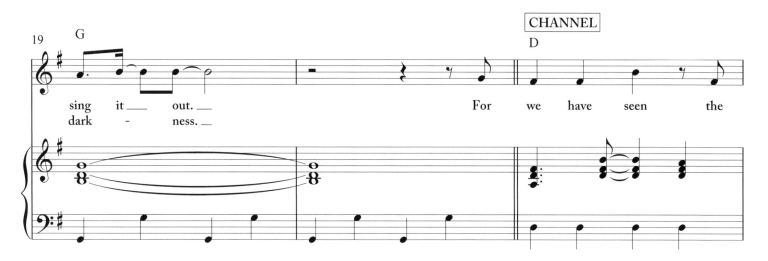

CHANNEL

sing it ___ out. ___ For we have seen the
dark - ness. ___

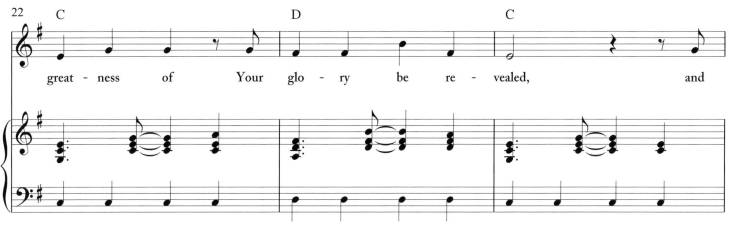

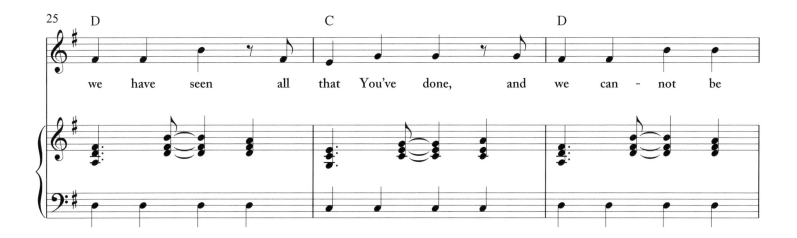

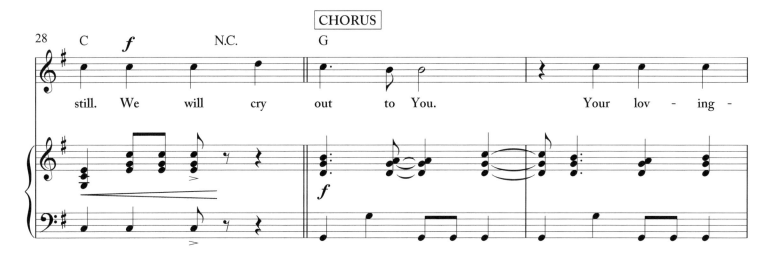

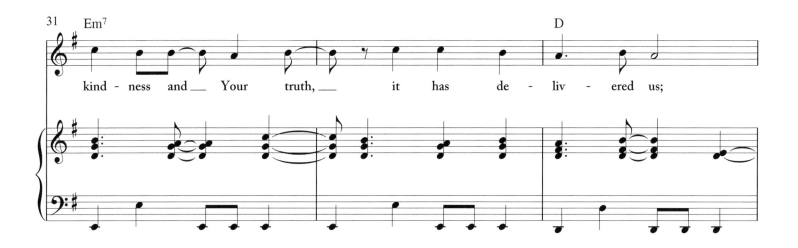

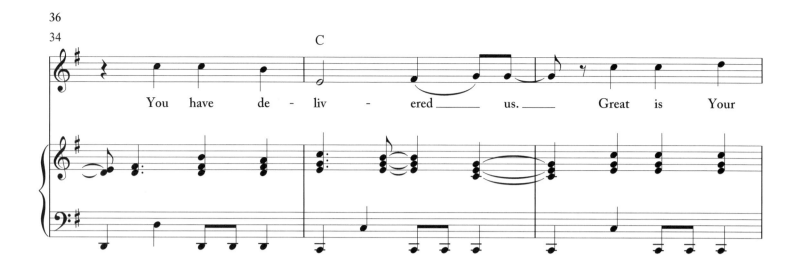

You have de - liv - ered _____ us. _____ Great is Your

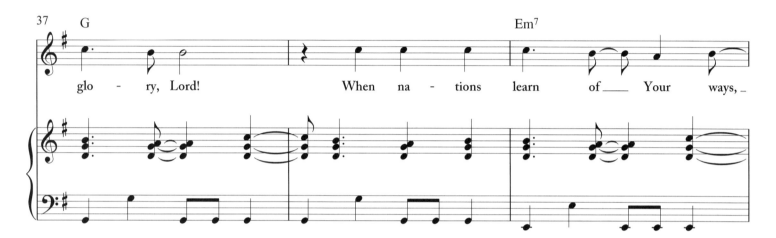

glo - ry, Lord! When na - tions learn of _____ Your ways, _

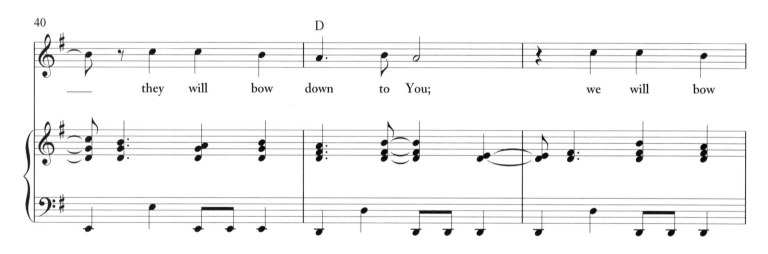

_____ they will bow down to You; we will bow

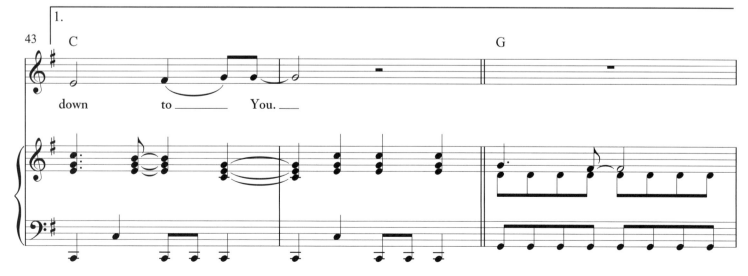

down to _____ You. _____

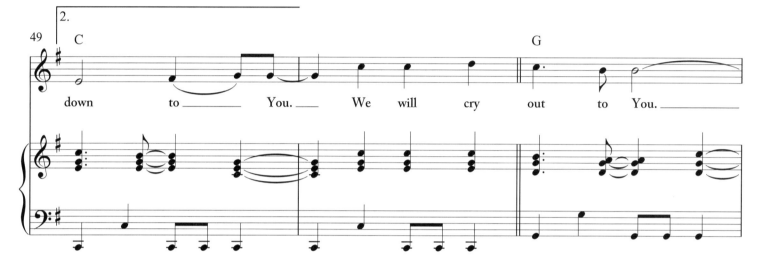

down to _____ You. ____ We will cry out to You. _____

Oh, _____ You have de - liv -

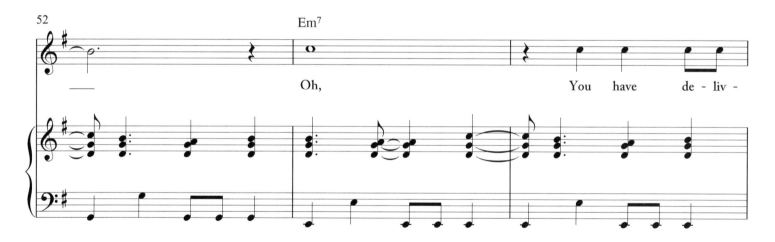

ered us, _____ You have de - liv - ered us. _____

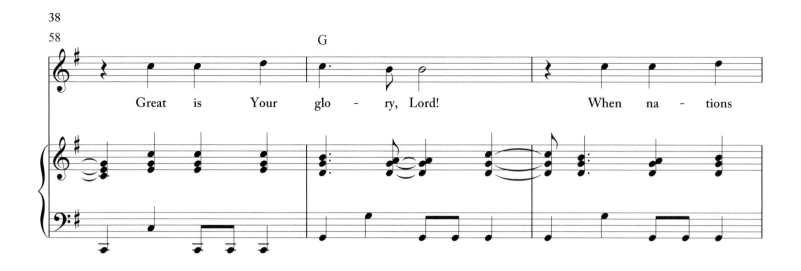

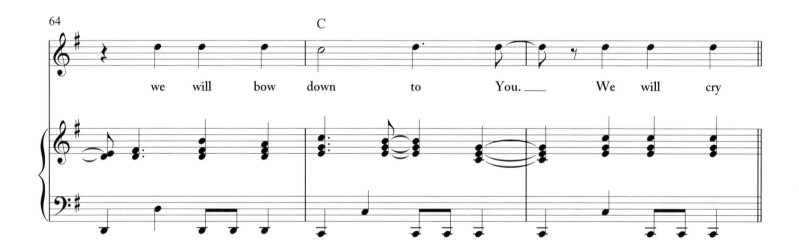

70

Great is___ Your glo - ry, Lord! _____

73

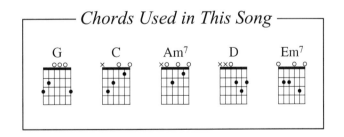

Chords Used in This Song

G   C   Am⁷   D   Em⁷

You Are the Lord

Words and Music by
JEREMY CAMP
and MATT MAHER

CHANNEL

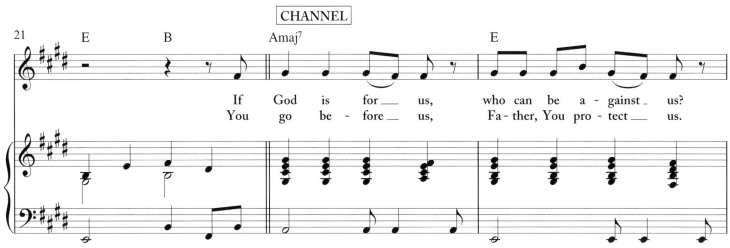

If God is for ___ us, who can be a - gainst ___ us?
You go be - fore ___ us, Fa - ther, You pro - tect ___ us.

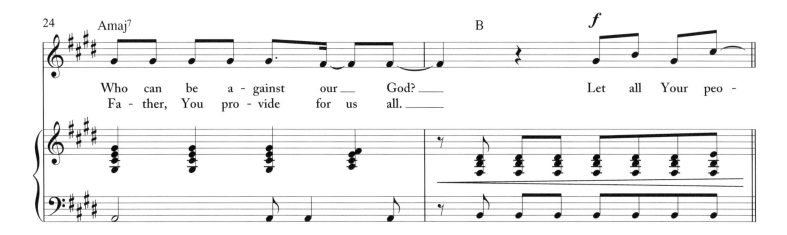

Who can be a - gainst our ___ God? ___ Let all Your peo -
Fa - ther, You pro - vide for us all. _____

CHORUS

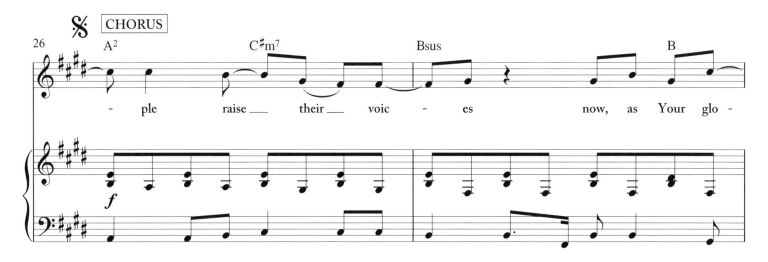

- ple raise ___ their ___ voic - es now, as Your glo -

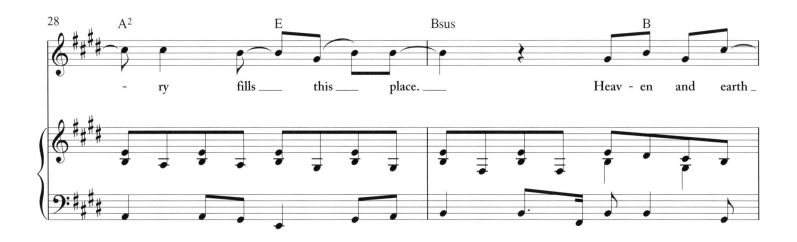

- ry fills ___ this ___ place. ___ Heav - en and earth ___

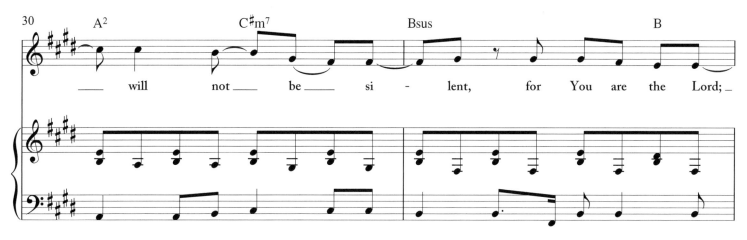

will not be si - lent, for You are the Lord; __

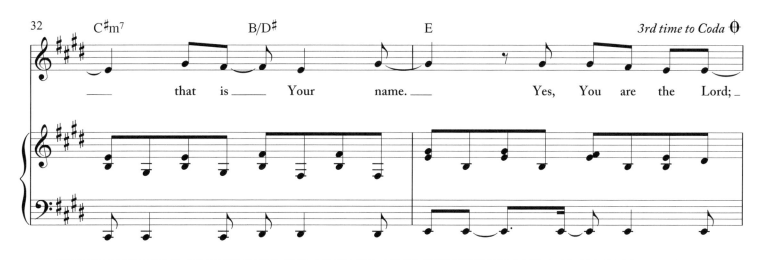

that is __ Your name. __ Yes, You are the Lord; __

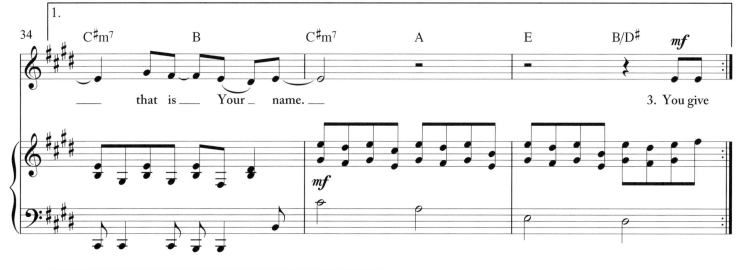

1.

that is __ Your __ name. __ 3. You give

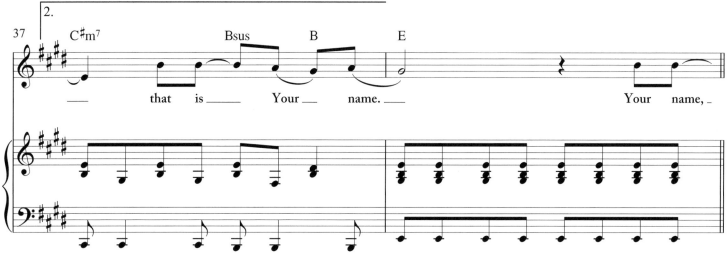

2.

that is __ Your __ name. __ Your name, __

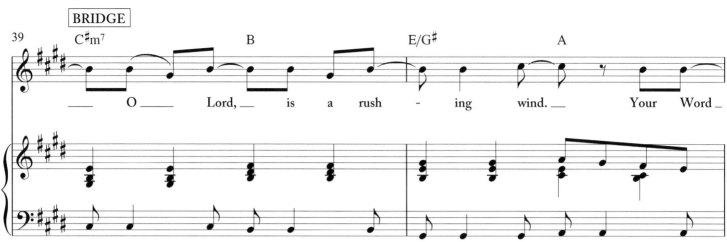

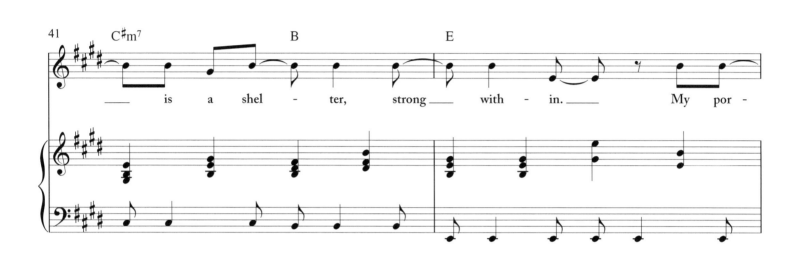

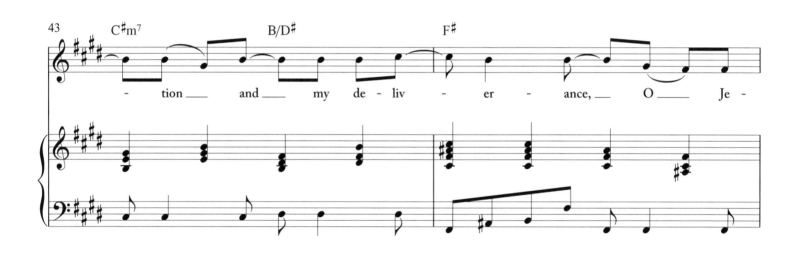

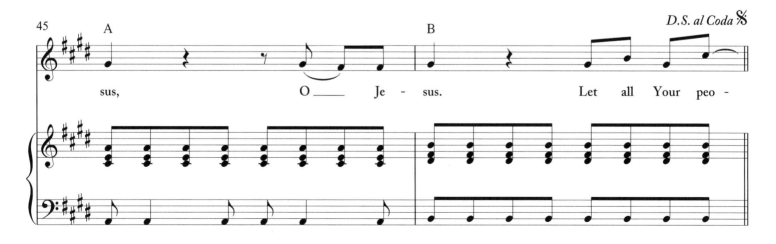

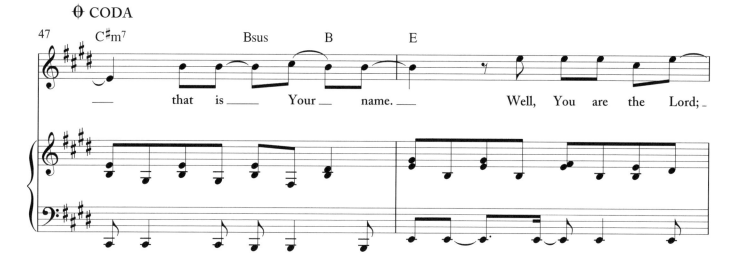

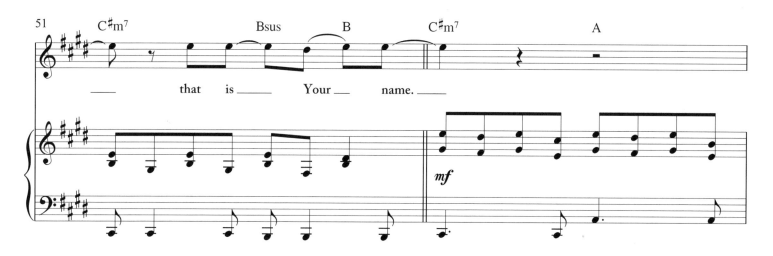

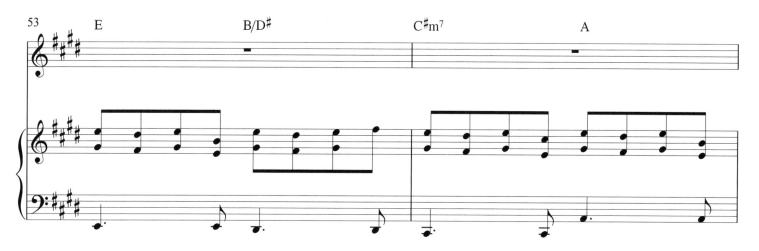

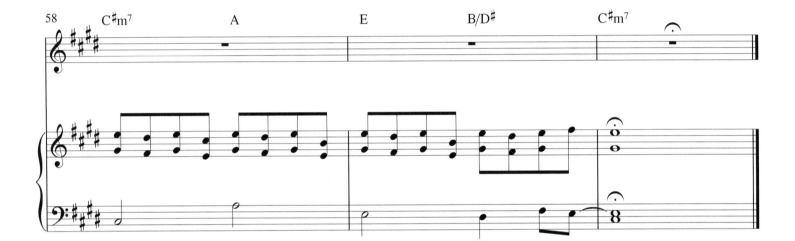

Chords Used in This Song

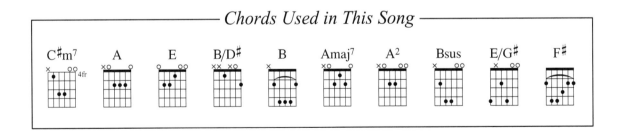

Everlasting God

Words and Music by
BRENTON BROWN
and KEN RILEY

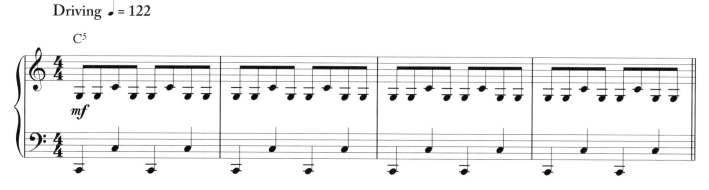

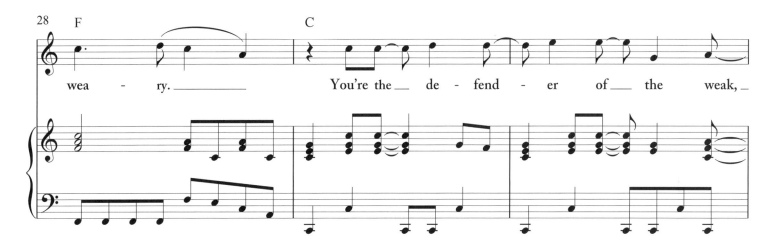

You com - fort those_ in need._ You lift_

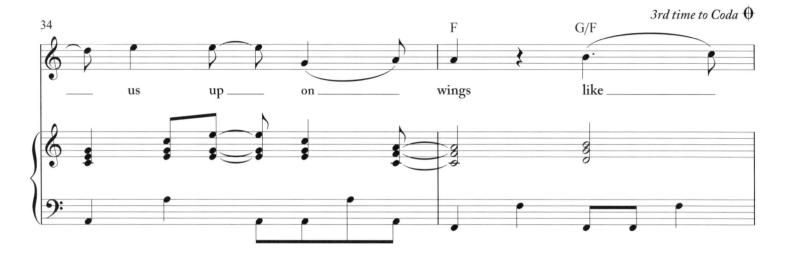

_ us up _ on _ wings like _

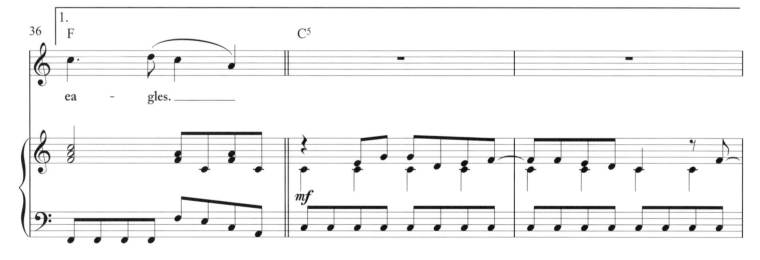

ea - gles. _

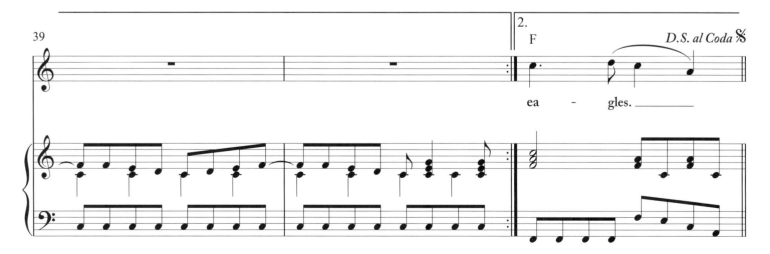

ea - gles. _

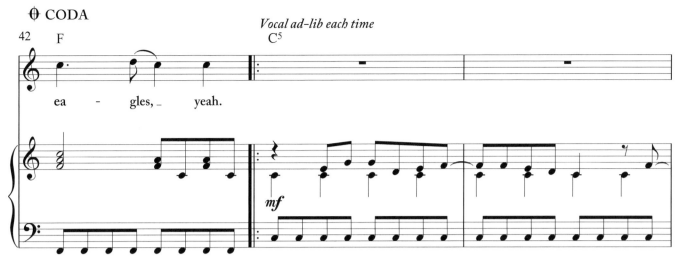

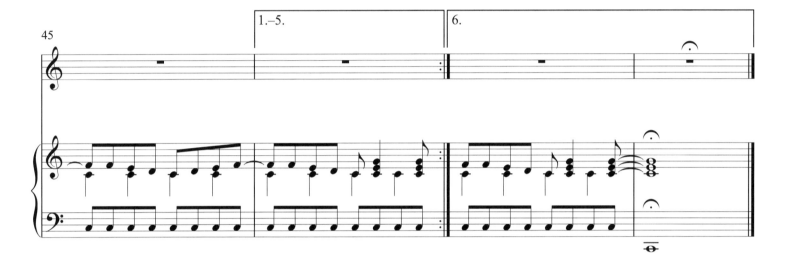

Chords Used in This Song

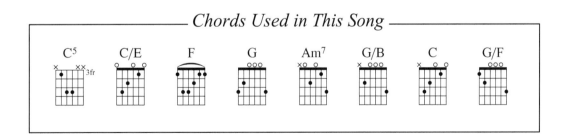

Overcome

Words and Music by
JON EGAN

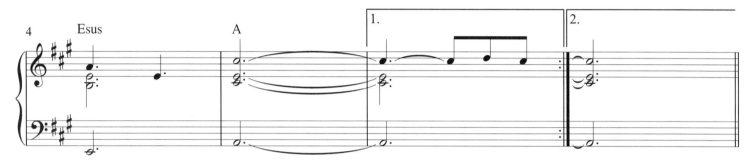

VERSE 1

1. Seat - ed a - bove, ___ en - throned in the Fa - ther's love; ___

des - tined to die, ___ poured out for all man -

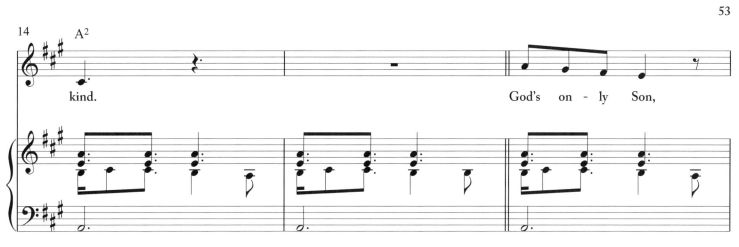

God's on - ly Son,

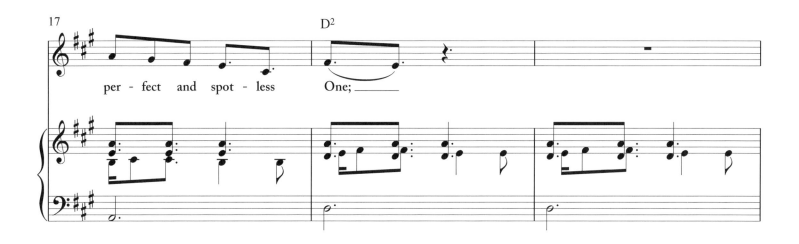

per - fect and spot - less One; _____

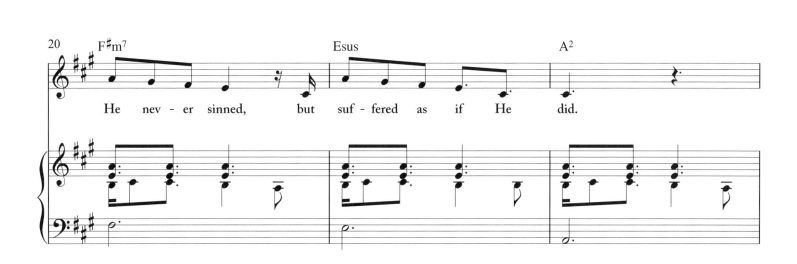

He nev - er sinned, but suf - fered as if He did.

CHANNEL

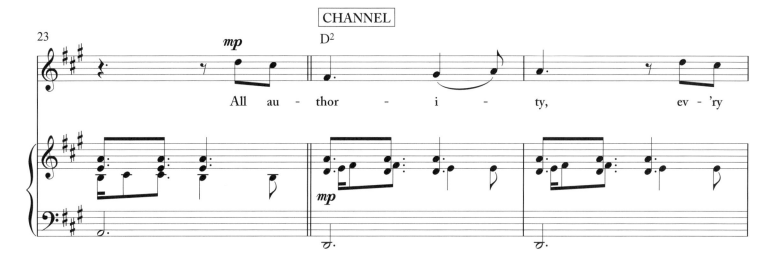

All au - thor - i - ty, ev - 'ry

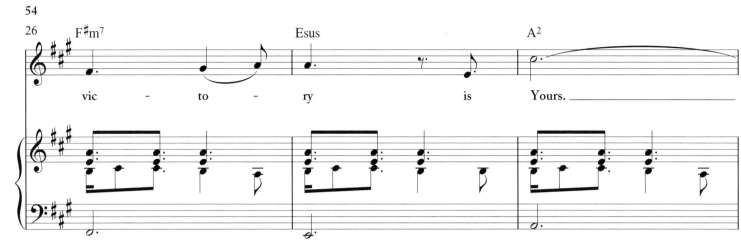

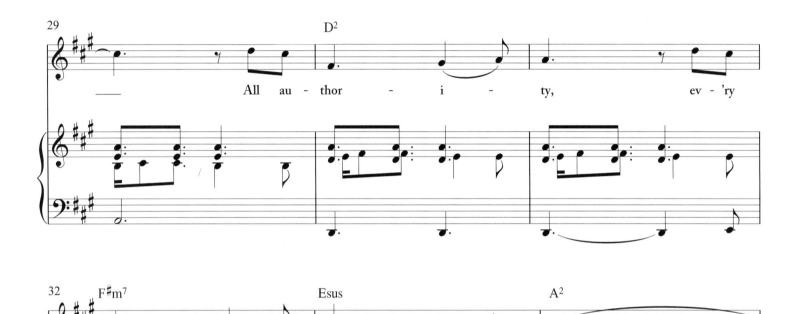

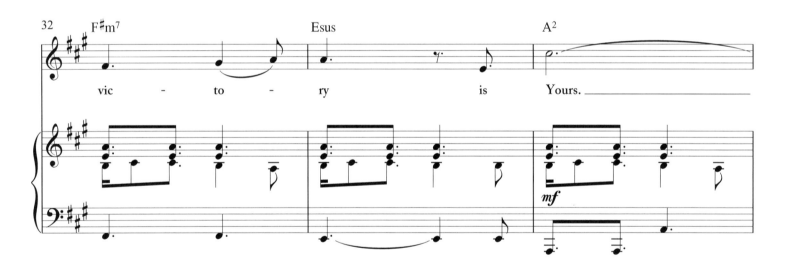

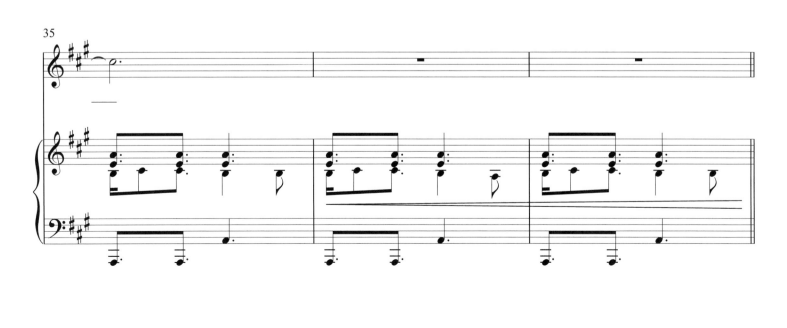

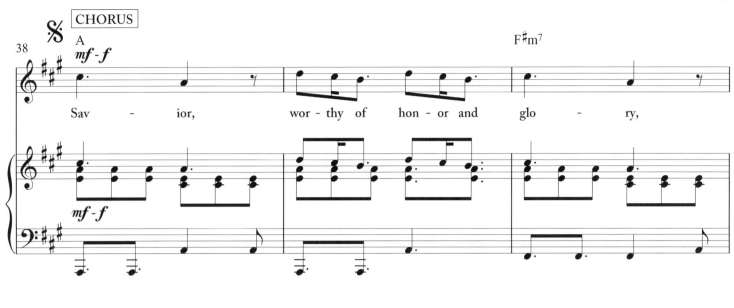

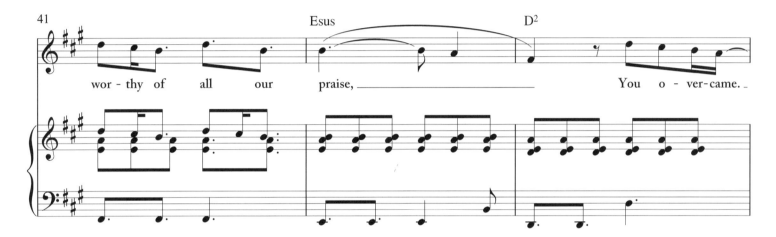

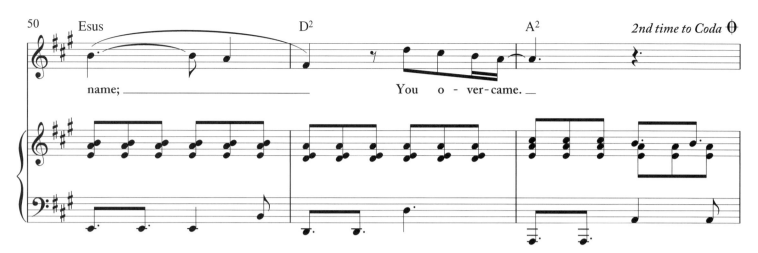

name; _____ You o - ver-came. _____

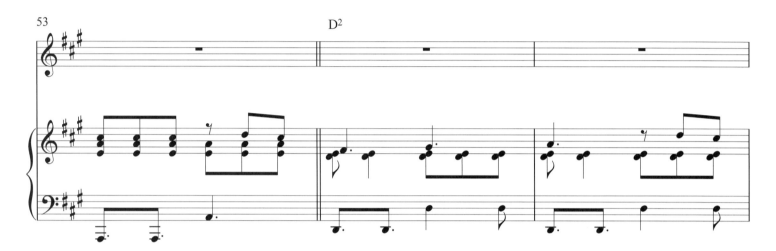

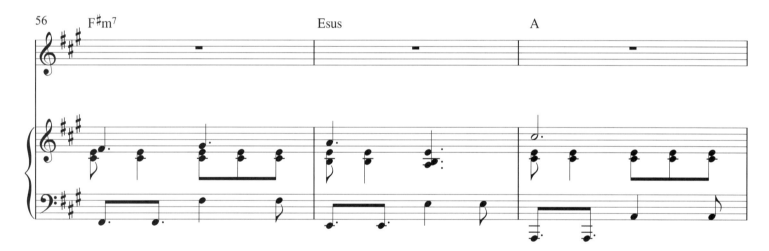

VERSE 2

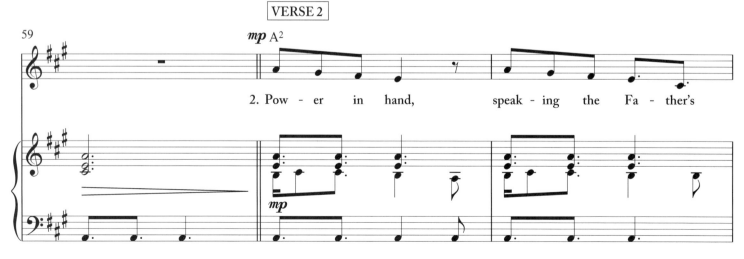

2. Pow - er in hand, speak - ing the Fa - ther's

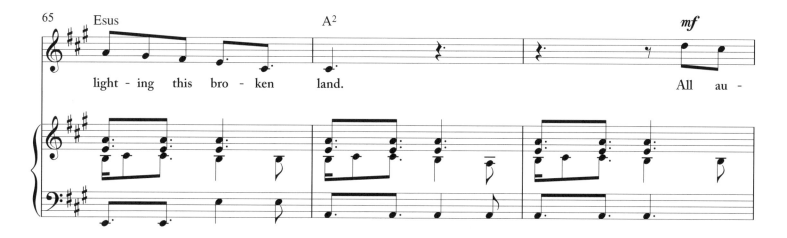

CHANNEL

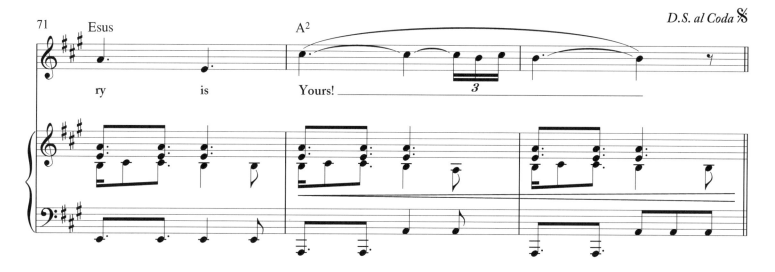

$\oplus$ CODA   **BRIDGE**

We will o - ver - come by the blood

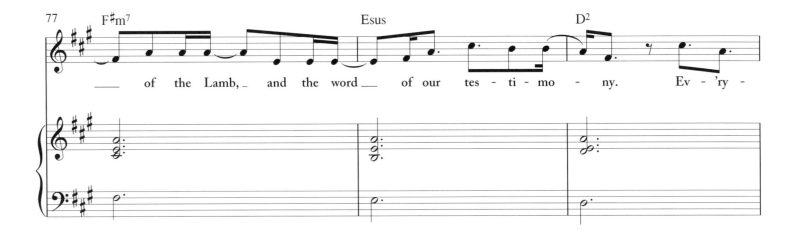

of the Lamb, and the word of our tes - ti - mo - ny. Ev - 'ry -

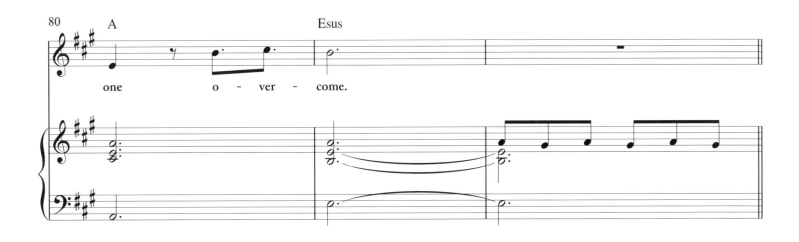

one o - ver - come.

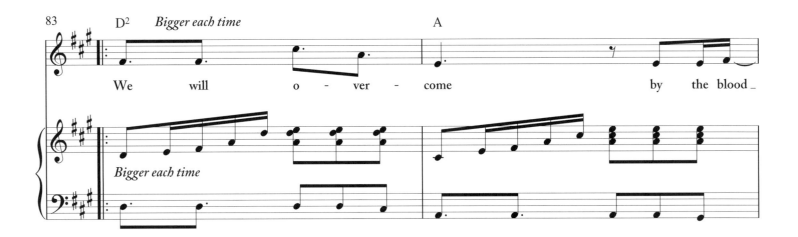

Bigger each time

We will o - ver - come by the blood

Bigger each time

of the Lamb ___ and the word ___ of our tes - ti - mo -

- ny. Ev - 'ry - one o - ver - come! ___

CHORUS

Repeat two times **ff**

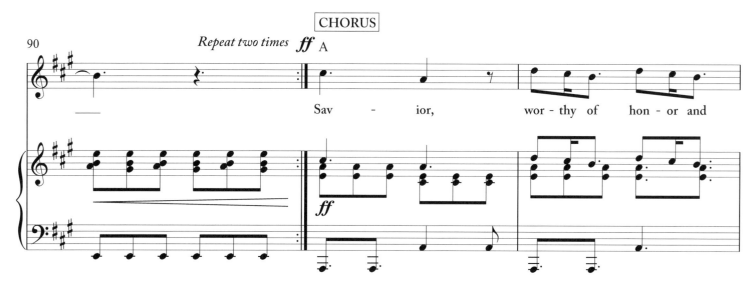

Sav - ior, wor - thy of hon - or and

glo - ry, wor - thy of all our praise, ___

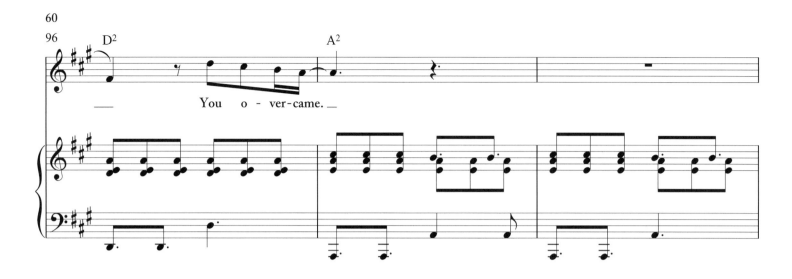

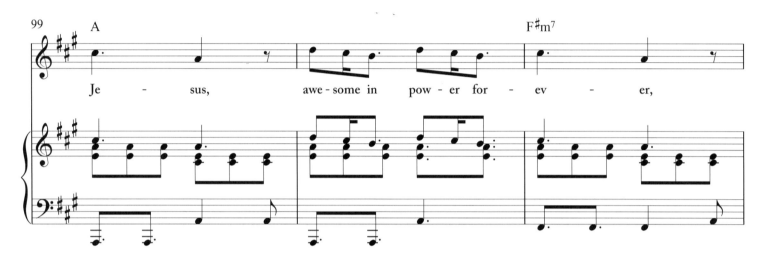

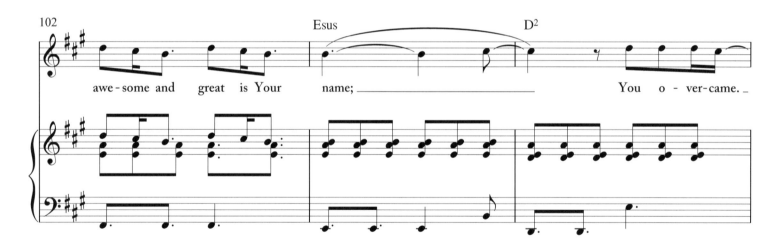

You o-ver-came! __ You o-ver-came! __

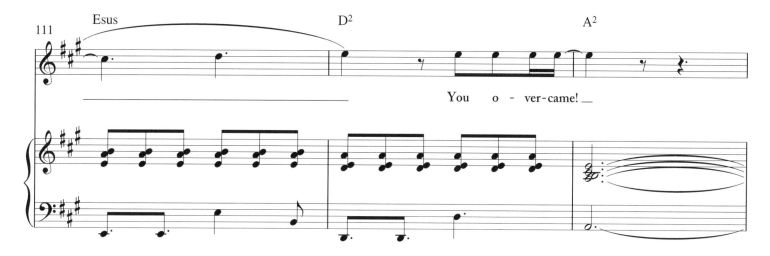

You o-ver-came! __

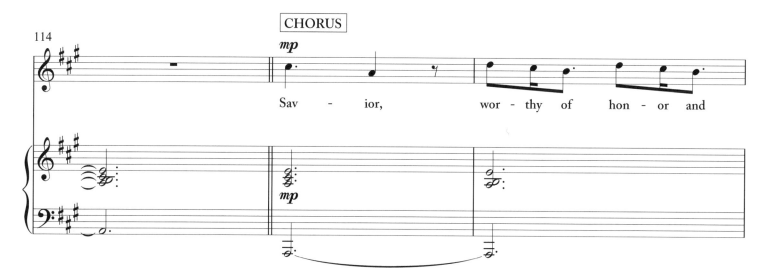

CHORUS

Sav - ior, wor - thy of hon - or and

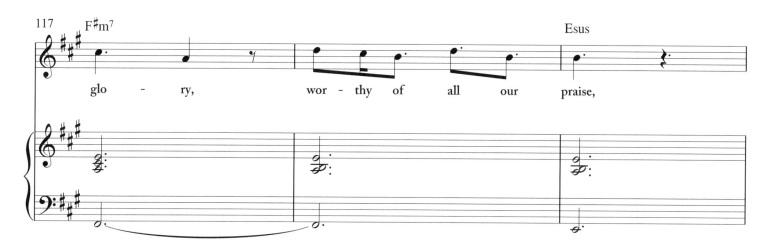

glo - ry, wor - thy of all our praise,

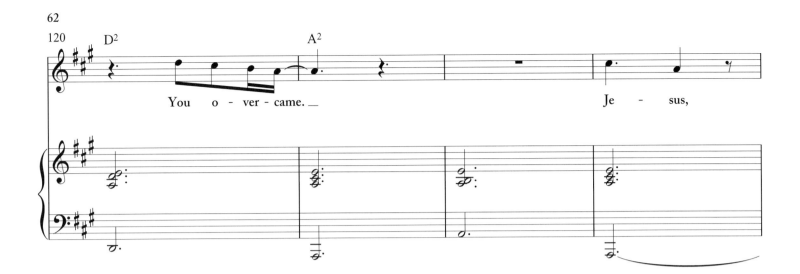

You o - ver - came. __ Je - sus,

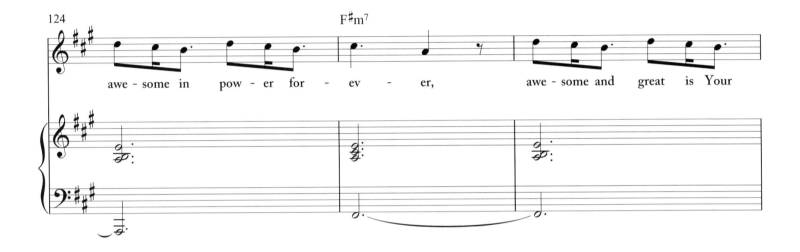

awe - some in pow - er for - ev - er, awe - some and great is Your

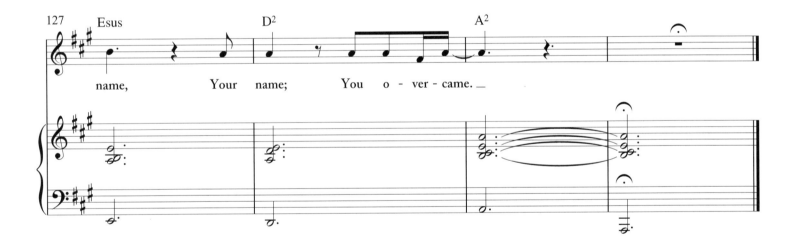

name, Your name; You o - ver - came. __

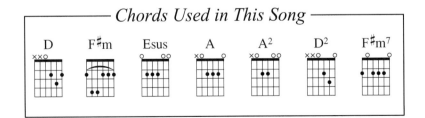

Chords Used in This Song

D   F♯m   Esus   A   A²   D²   F♯m⁷

You Never Let Go

Capo 3 (G)

Words and Music by
MATT REDMAN
and BETH REDMAN

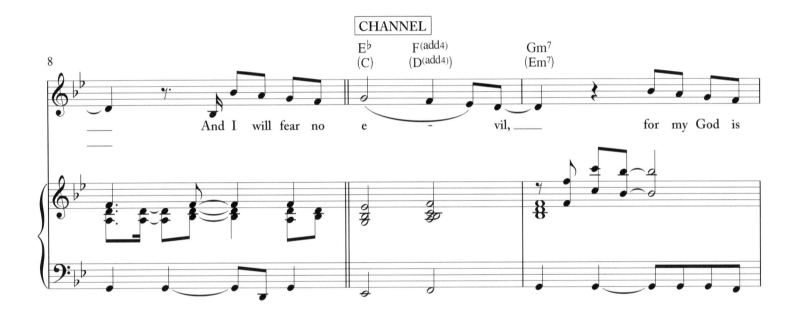

CHORUS

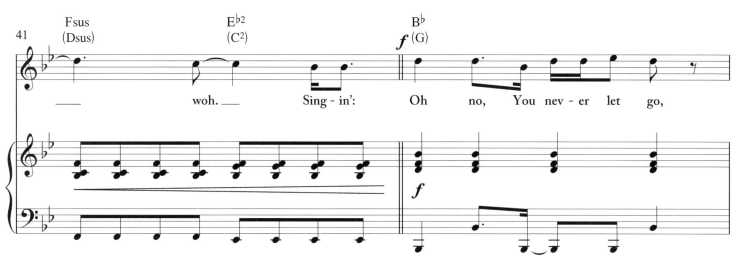

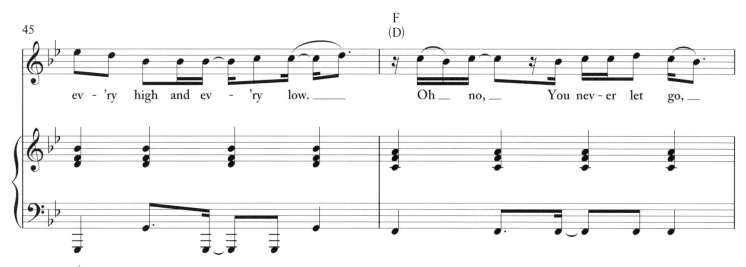

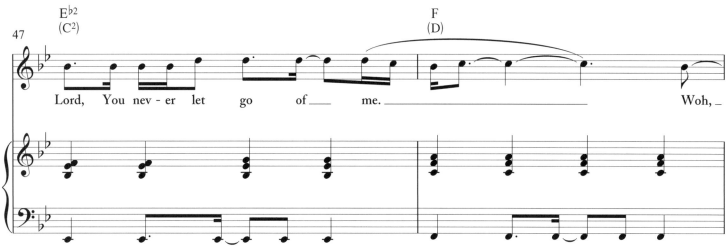

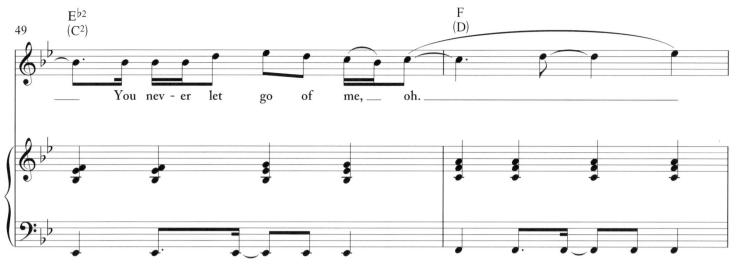

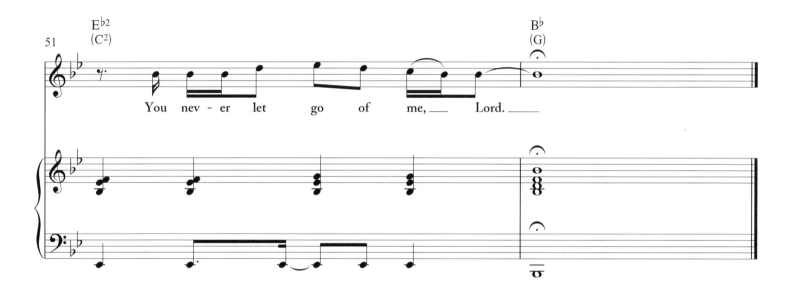

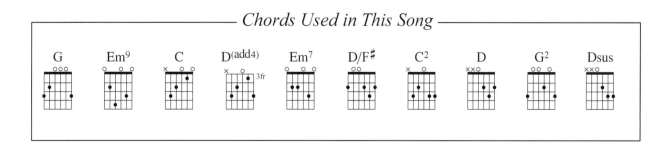

Unrestrained

Words and Music by
JEREMY CAMP

Smoothly ♩ = 82

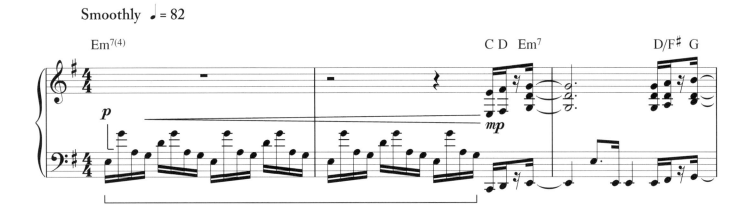

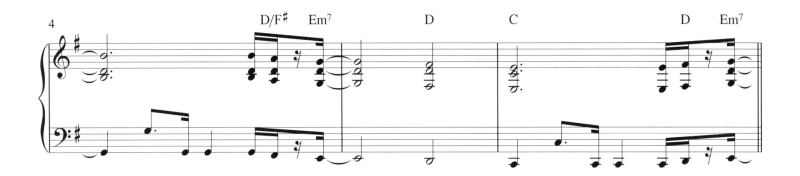

VERSE

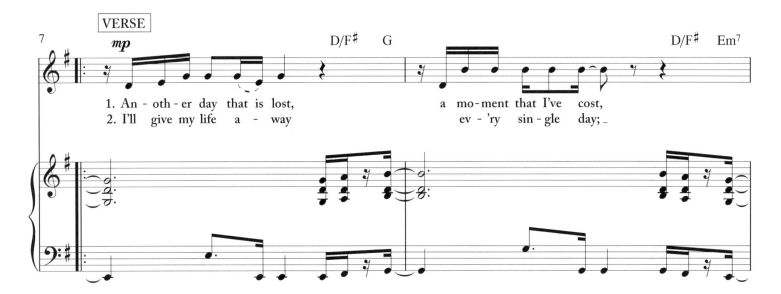

1. An-oth-er day that is lost,   a mo-ment that I've cost,
2. I'll give my life a-way   ev-'ry sin-gle day;

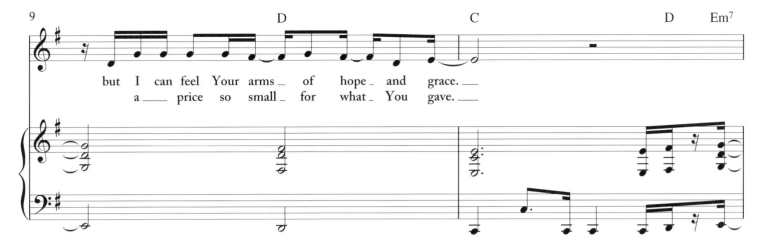

but I can feel Your arms of hope and grace.
a price so small for what You gave.

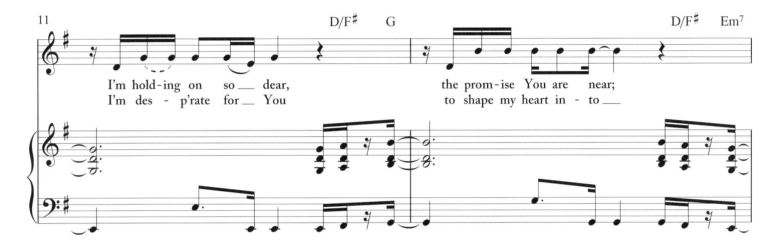

I'm hold-ing on so dear, the prom-ise You are near;
I'm des - p'rate for You to shape my heart in - to

Your lov-ing-kind - ness nev - er fails. So take
the ver - y im - age of what I'm to be.

CHORUS

this self - ish heart of mine. I want to give it all;

I've wast-ed too __ much time. __ And melt __ a - way __

ev - 'ry-thing that's not __ of You. __ I want to know You __ more, __

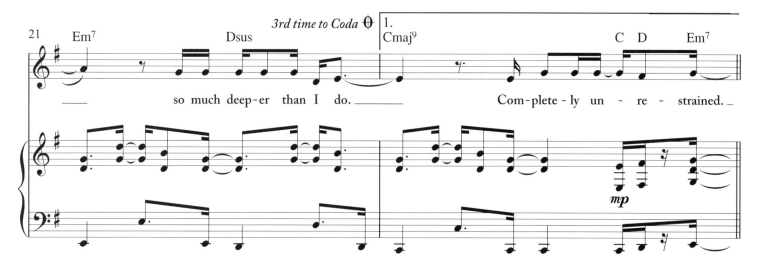

3rd time to Coda

so much deep-er than I do. __ Com - plete - ly un - re - strained. __

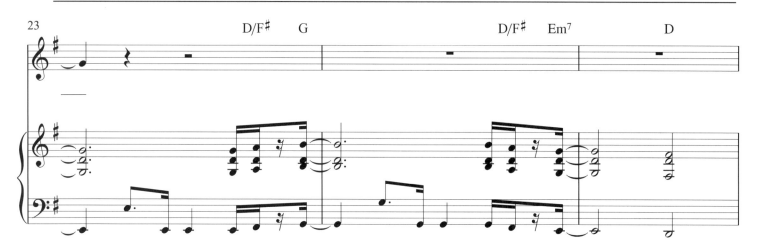

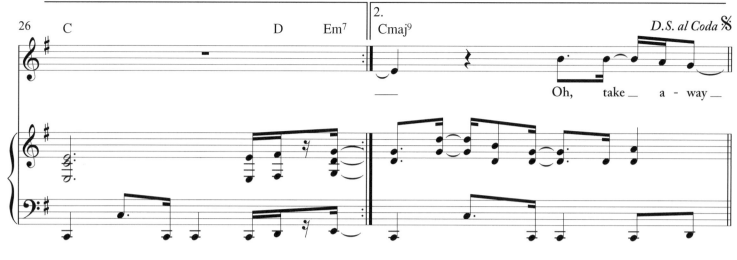

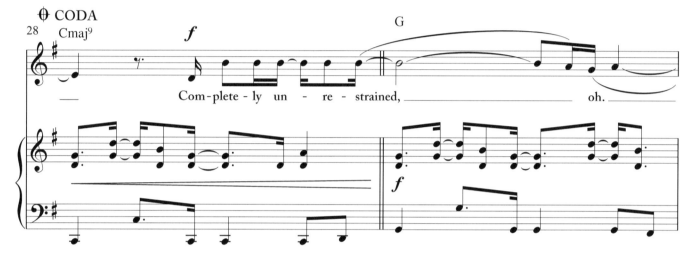

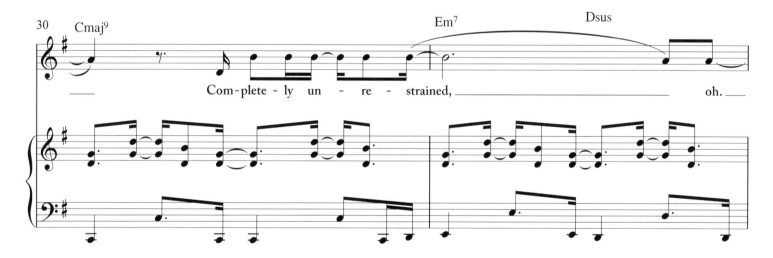

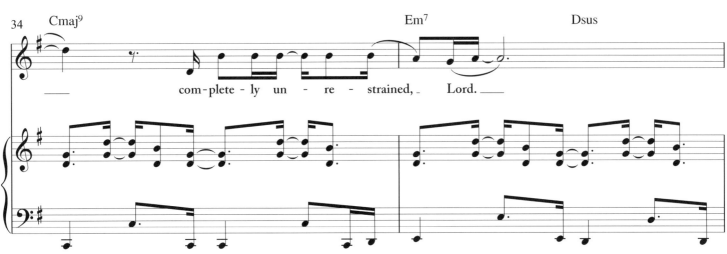

Chords Used in This Song

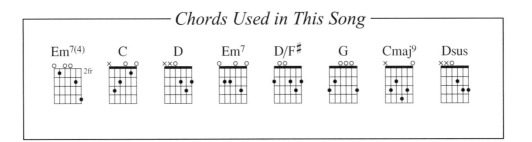

King Jesus

Words and Music by
JEREMY CAMP

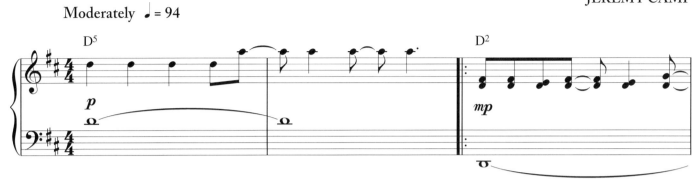

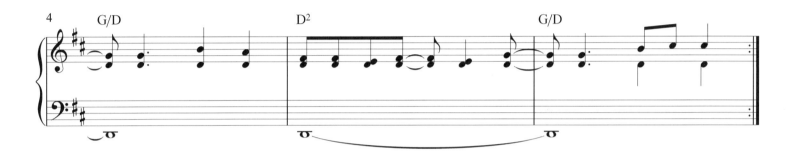

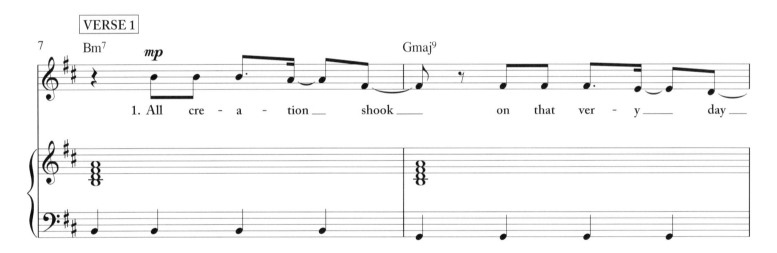

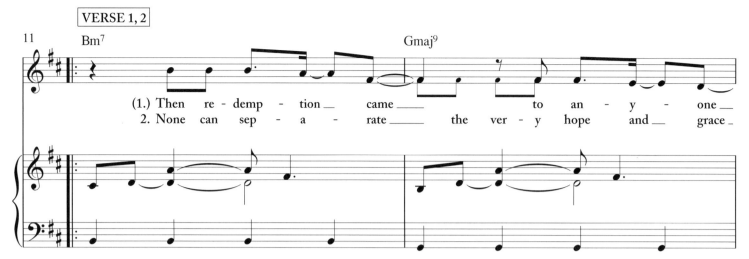

VERSE 1, 2

(1.) Then re - demp - tion ___ came ___ to an - y - one ___
2. None can sep - a - rate ___ the ver - y hope and ___ grace _

___ who would call His ___ name. ___
___ that He dis - played. ___

With pow - er and with ___ strength, ___ You broke these heav - y ___ chains, ___
Nei - ther height, nor ___ depth, ___ nor an - y - one ___

___ and sal - va - tion ___ reigned. ___ And with a
___ can steal the love He ___ gave. ___

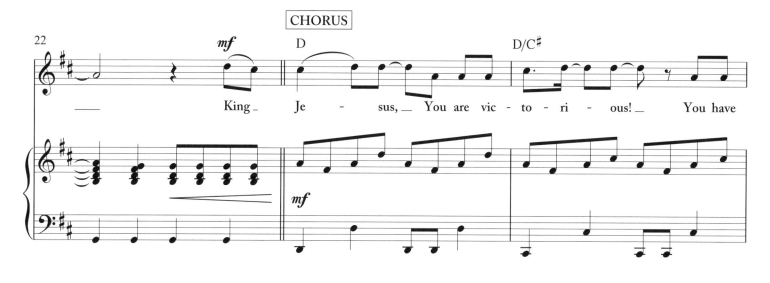

CHORUS

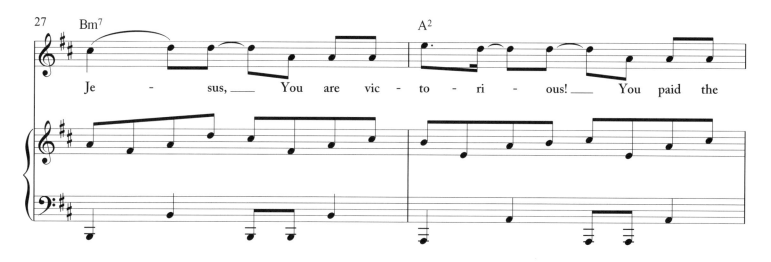

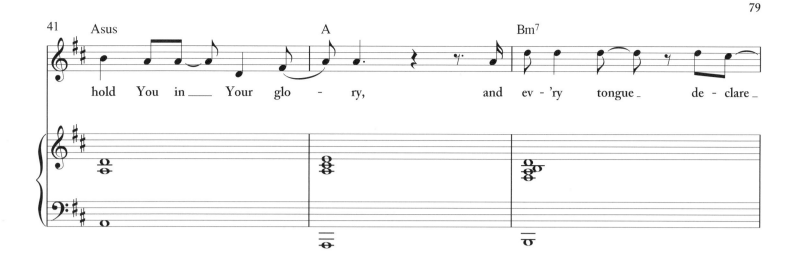

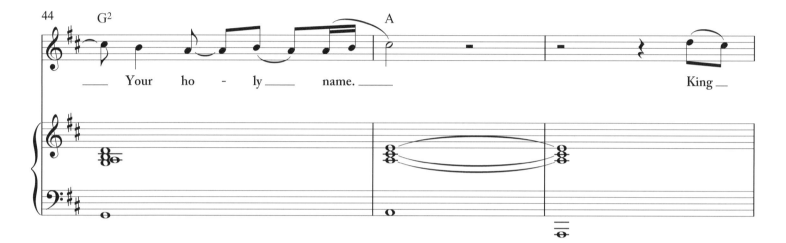

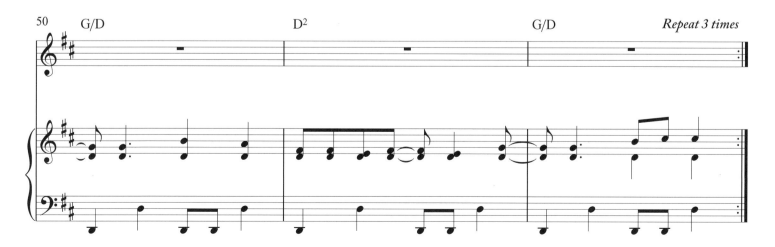

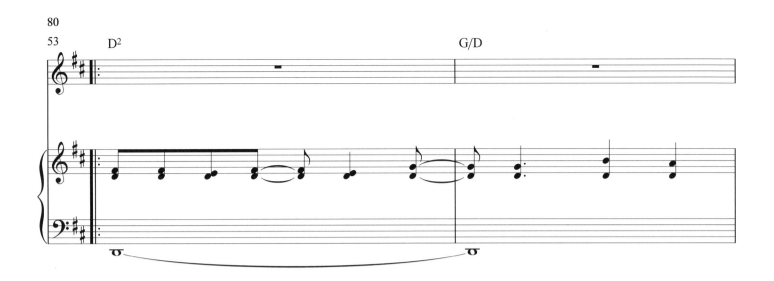

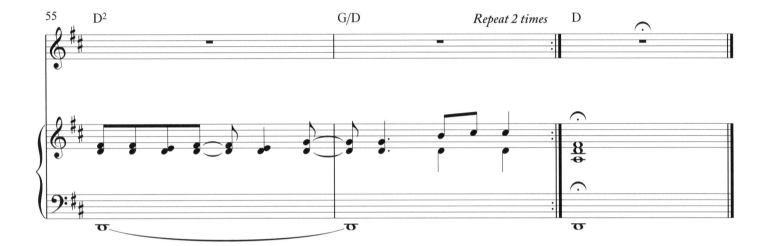

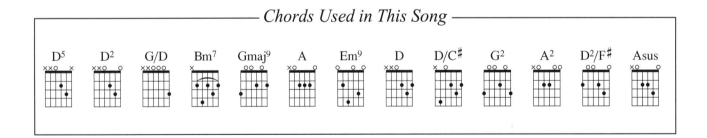

Chords Used in This Song